Deichman Bjørvika Oslo Public Library

Deichman Bjørvika Oslo Public Library

Lundhagem and Atelier Oslo Architects

Edited by
Lars Müller and the architects

Texts by
Niklas Maak
Elif Shafak
Liv Sæteren

Photographs by
Einar Aslaksen
Iwan Baan
Hélène Binet

Lars Müller Publishers

Preface

One spring day in 2009 we received the fantastic news that we had won the international architectural competition to design the new main library in our own hometown. Little did we know then of the process that lay ahead, or that it would take eleven years before we saw the public entering the finished library and putting it to use.

The architectural competition called for a vision of the library of the future, a redefinition of what a modern public library could be. These ambitions encouraged us to ask fundamental questions about the role of architecture and how we could create a meaningful space that could be adapted to future needs we didn't even know what would be.

Our core ambitions and ideas as presented to the competition jury have survived through the entire process, but have also undergone further development in a unique collaboration between the two architectural offices, librarians, project leaders, consultants, and contractors. The project has faced many challenges on the way, from difficult ground conditions to political changes, but at the same time we have enjoyed support and help from very many productive internal and external collaborators who have aided the project in numerous ways.

This book is an attempt to summarize that process in order to provide a better understanding of how the library was conceived and developed, how architects work, and how a building such as this comes into being. Three texts written specially for this book place the building in an historical and civic context. Elif Shafak reminds us of what libraries have meant and may mean for society. Liv Sæteren shares the story of how the public library as an institution was developed and how the Nordic countries played a leading role in the development of libraries. Niklas Maak views the project from an external point of view and places it in a wider architectural and ideological context. Photographs by Hélène Binet, Iwan Baan and Einar Aslaksen convey the physical shapes and spaces of the building, but also life as it is lived and breathed in the library.

It has been a relief and a great joy to see that the public are drawn to the library and how well they enjoy it. Along with the wonderful content and activities instigated by the librarians it has become an exciting and vibrant place for the whole city to use.

Lundhagem and Atelier Oslo, architects for Deichman Bjørvika

Home Is Inside a Library

Elif Shafak

There is no better place for lonely children than a library.

Whatever our age and occupation, there is no sanctuary in the world more peaceful, restorative and nurturing than a library.

I did not grow up in a house full of books. As a child in Turkey, in my grandmother's simple and modest place, I had no idea that some homes proudly displayed floor-to-ceiling libraries and wooden ladders that could be moved to any point to reach the upper shelves. I had no idea that there were private residences that resembled shrines dedicated to books, and you could read and keep reading all your life, and still not be able to finish all the titles under your roof. Nor had I come across a public library – not yet.

But I did grow up in a house full of stories. Folktales, fables, myths, legends. Traditional narratives of the Middle East, Anatolia, the Balkans, the Black Sea, the Mediterranean and the Levant. Oral storytelling – both ancient and modern. The tales I heard from Grandma were like rich tapestries woven with silk threads in the brightest colors and most dazzling designs. Grandma's stories were almost always replete with adventures, odysseys, striking personalities, unlikely heroes and thrilling happenings. Even so, I noticed two surprising qualities about them: that they changed each time they were repeated, depending on the size of the audience or the mood of the storyteller, and that, no matter how short or long the story, there were always subtle pauses in between sentences, gaps scattered along the arc of the plot, empty spaces hidden amidst words. Grandma was a brilliant storyteller, but I couldn't help wondering if there were things she preferred not to tell, and if so, what could be the reason? I started to pay more attention to the absences nestled inside narratives – to both what was said and what was left unsaid, untouched, unasked. I became interested not only in stories but also in silences – and over time, I became more and more drawn to those who have been silenced, marginalized, disempowered, pushed to the periphery of the society.

A storyteller, every storyteller, is perhaps an explorer of silences.

Literature is an act of resistance to render the invisible more visible, the unheard more heard, and ultimately, to rehumanize those who have been dehumanized.

Silences were important to me from the very beginning, and there were many of them in my life. I was an only child raised by a single mother who worked long hours away from home and a superstitious grandmother who spent a considerable part of her days speaking to invisible creatures. Many mornings when I woke up I would find Grandma sitting by the window with a coffee cup in her hand, nodding her head to the quiet around the house, which she said was not quiet at all, but thick with conversations and discussions. They were talkative like that, the djinn. I pricked my ears, I tried so hard, but I couldn't hear them.

It is not like there were no books in Grandma's house. There were. A few. The love story of Laila and Majnun, the love story of Khosrow and Shirin, a thick tome of Islamic Interpretation of Dreams to be consulted after each dream and nightmare, the jokes and wise teachings of Nasruddin Hodja, poems by Rabindranath Tagore, a copy of *One Thousand and One Nights,* and various strange volumes on wild herbs, edible flowers and medicinal plants. Grandma was a healer, and people came from near and far to see her – people with skin diseases, people suffering from asthma, people with anxiety disorders, depression and melancholy. With utmost kindness, she offered them homemade lotions and balms, ointments and potions for free, but mostly, she spoke to them and they listened to her.

"Words have power," I thought to myself as I observed her silently from a corner.

There was also a Qur'an in the house, but it was up on the wall, encased in a beautiful, pearlescent sheath, and it somehow felt beyond reach. Still, I liked to take the Holy Book every now and then, and ask endless questions about God, creation, vice and virtue, hell and heaven. I was particularly interested in Adam and Eve – and that infamous apple tree – trying to comprehend why Eve got all the blame for the couple's sudden exile from paradise.

My questions came to an abrupt end when I was explicitly told, not by Grandma, who was a compassionate and loving woman, but by some of the neighbors and "patients" who visited our house, that a girl should not touch the Holy Book whenever she pleased. It would take me a while to understand what exactly they meant by that. According to these people, girls, once they started having their periods, could never be regarded as "clean" as boys. This cultural teaching offended me profoundly. Apparently, men could open the Holy Book whenever they wanted. All they needed was to wash their hands beforehand. Women could not do so even if they were to take a full bath, because for an entire week every month, they were deemed to be "dirty."

Unconvinced and upset, I looked up the definition of the word *dirty* in the Turkish dictionary. I found two separate meanings in there. The first meaning was the usual one: unclean. But the second meaning made me pause, and then it made me angry. The Turkish dictionary claimed that dirty also meant: "a woman who is menstruating."

Until then, thanks to Grandma's stories and superstitions, I had discovered at an early age that words were magical and powerful. But I had never known that words could also hurt.

We live in an age where there is an abundance of information, but very little knowledge, and even less wisdom. These three concepts, although at times used interchangeably, are completely different things.

Too much information prompts fast consumption. Cursory, speedy. The truth is we cannot process such a huge load of information, so we just let it slide over our heads. Every day, almost mechanically, we scroll up and down our social media feeds, picking bits and pieces of news here and there. But this does not constitute knowledge. In fact, the continuous overflow of information can even be an obstacle in front of attaining proper knowledge. Our easy and effortless access to all kinds of information gives us the impression that we "know" a thing or two about every subject, including the most random topics. However, true knowledge is hard work. It requires time, attention, patience, accumulation, self-doubt, a nuanced way of thinking, cognitive flexibility and also, humility.... Knowledge asks us to slow down because it cannot be rushed. Knowledge advises us to be humble, making us realize that no matter how much we think we know, there is so much more we are yet to learn.

Today, bombarded with capsules of information – as well as disinformation – we have almost forgotten how to say "I don't know." We do not utter these three words often, if at all. When was the last time we ever said "I don't know" to anyone – unless we are speaking to younger children, in which case we might – just might – be willing to accept our ignorance on certain subjects only to indicate that certain subjects are complicated by nature. But between adults, we like to keep up the appearance of being "knowledgeable," and if there is a theme we are not really familiar with, well, we can simply Google it. It only takes a few minutes, doesn't it? But once again, that is not knowledge.

Knowledge requires books. Continuous reading. Slow journalism. Investigative research. In-depth analysis. A critical way of thinking that is not only open to infinite learning but also averse to rigid certainties, entrenched dogmas and absolutist convictions.

Knowledge is a delicate ecosystem with all its roots and branches and leaves, and it is nurtured in libraries.

And then there is wisdom, which is as rare as red rubies. Wisdom asks us to bring the mind and the heart together. It blends rational intelligence with emotional sagacity. It thrives upon empathy. Wisdom needs art, literature, culture, compassion, humor, freedom of speech and an innate respect for humanity in all its multiplicity and diversity. It also involves the ability to put ourselves in the shoes of another person, even if for a few hours or days.

Wisdom, too, lives inside libraries.

How can we ever change the triple ratio of "too much information, too little knowledge and even less wisdom" that characterizes our world today? How can we increase knowledge and grow wisdom but consciously decrease this relentless deluge of drops of information raining on our heads every single day? How can we slow down this restless flow of news that blinds our vision, dulls our minds, fatigues our bodies and eventually, numbs our hearts by plunging us into apathy?

To rectify the long-broken proportion of information to knowledge and wisdom, we need our public libraries.

My first encounter with a library was at school in Ankara. This was a simple, chunky wooden cupboard tucked in a corner of the classroom with a hanging sign that said "Class Library – Do Not Touch!"

Inside there were numerous titles, mostly Western classics and Turkish children's stories, neatly arranged and lined up behind a glass case, which remained locked during the day. At the end of every week the student who had earned five golden stickers from the teacher was given the right to borrow a book. We were forty-two kids in that classroom and there weren't enough stickers. There weren't even enough books. Still, I didn't care. I worked so hard to make sure those glass doors could be unlocked!

Behind the glass doors were Victor Hugo's *Les Misérables*, *A Tale of Two Cities* by Charles Dickens, various books on Ottoman history and

Ataturk, the founder of modern Turkey, Gogol's *Dead Souls,* Honoré de Balzac's *Lost Illusions,* Dostoyevski's *The Brothers Karamazov,* Knut Hamsun's *Hunger,* Miguel de Cervantes's *Don Quixote,* Mark Twain's *The Adventures of Tom Sawyer....* I read them all. Over the years, I read them again and again. Life was boring. Days felt repetitive. Our teacher put restrictions on the number of titles we could take home with us. She did not seem to understand how much I needed books to survive.

So, out of necessity, I started to mix stories in my mind. I blended the Eastern tales I found in my Grandma's house with the Western novels available at the school library. Beautiful and brave Laila, tired of Majnun's endless infatuation with her, would show up in a small town near Moscow to discuss philosophical questions on free will, divine justice and moral responsibility with Ivan Fyodorovich Karamazov. I would imagine Nasruddin Hodja, a Sufi with a great sense of humor and a sharp mind, chatting with Huckleberry Finn along the Mississippi River, then embarking on a journey to Bengal to absorb the poetry and philosophy of Tagore. I would dream of a concubine in the Ottoman Empire escaping the harem and managing to travel to Paris in the nineteenth century to meet the charismatic ex-convict Jean Valjean.

I loved it when fictional characters left their own stories and walked into other people's stories. Unlike in real life, there were no impermeable boundaries in the vast kingdom of Storyland. No national borders. No wired fences. No passport controls or police vans. I treasured that sense of mobility, peripatetic freedom. Perhaps I needed to be assured that geographical frontiers, no matter how strictly drawn, could be transcended. I needed to see that with the help of stories one could voyage far and beyond, even travel the entire world. It was books that taught me this possibility – all the books that I could get my hands on in that small, conservative neighborhood in Ankara.

Connecting cultures and places was important to me not only to make sense of the world around but also to grasp who I was. You see, I was born in France, Strasbourg, to Turkish parents. My first home was a sunlit flat in a banlieue, a house full of immigrants, university students, mostly leftists, smoking Gauloises, dreaming of a revolution, reading Louis Althusser and Jean-Paul Sartre (but not so much Simone de Beauvoir). There were books everywhere in my first home. Books were shared, discussed, circulated among friends. Books were like song-birds that could never stand still – they regularly migrated from one reader to the next.

Later on, my parents separated. My father stayed in France and married again. I would not see him for many years, and I would not meet my half-brothers until I would reach my mid-twenties.

Meanwhile my mother brought me to Ankara. For her, Turkey was "motherland." For me, however, it was a completely new country where I felt uprooted, de-rooted, slightly lost. It was in this state that we arrived at my grandmother's home. A sage-green two-story house with a garden, located in the middle of a conservative, patriarchal environment. It was clear to me from the start that we did not fit in here. I did not fit in. If it weren't for stories and all the underground tunnels that I painstakingly dug to reach the open meadows of "Storyland," I would have felt trapped, confined. If it weren't for books, and that tiny library I found at school, I would lose my mind.

Over the years, I have written many chapters of my novels in various libraries around the world. When I first moved to Istanbul as an aspiring author, it was thanks to the city's old and new libraries that I was able to find a sense of belonging, a feeling of home – Beyazit Library, SALT Galata, A. H. Tanpinar Library.... It pained me to see how few libraries there were in a metropolis as vast and old as Istanbul. So much money and investment was poured into opening shopping mall after shopping mall, but there was no support whatsoever in local libraries. I have lived and written in Istanbul for many years, and she broke my heart like no other city ever could. Still today, miles away from Istanbul, I carry that She-city with me, lodged in my soul.

There are several libraries in other countries where I found refuge, where I read, wrote and imagined my stories: the fantastically gothic library at Mount Holyoke near Boston, the amazing Michigan Library, the impressive New York Public Library.... And then, after I moved to the UK, the great library of The Bodleian at Oxford or the London Library with its quiet desks and charming reading room.... The new Library in Oslo is is also among the libraries that are dearest to me.... In a world where knowledge is under attack, truth is systematically distorted and lies can be easily spread through digital technologies, every library you see is a little miracle, an oasis flourishing in the desert of ignorance.

One of Grandma's stories that I have never forgotten, despite all these years, was about a library in Baghdad in the thirteenth century. It was called The House of Wisdom. Rare books, collections of poetry in both Arabic and Persian, the private compendium of Caliph Harun al-Rashid.... All of them were destroyed during the siege of the city. So many books were thrown into the River Tigris that for days afterwards the water ran pitch-black. I still see it in my dreams sometimes – antique pages beautifully handwritten and illustrated with gold and silver, drowning in rivers of ink.

In the early 1990s, on this European continent, the National Library in Bosnia was attacked by a similar force of barbarism. The historic building was one of the most important hubs of culture and knowledge in this region, home to over 2 million volumes, 150,000 rare books. Targeted by incendiary grenades and snipers, the library began burning one midnight, and it did not stop burning for three days.

Among the librarians who tried to save books was a young woman, who was newly engaged. Her name was Aida Buturović. She was shot while trying to rescue rare books from the flames. She was incredibly brave, dedicated to her work. Writers and readers from all over the world, we owe her a debt of gratitude – we need to keep her name alive, repeat it all the time, Aida. We owe so much to every librarian whose story we might not yet know but who has gone out of their way to preserve culture and knowledge, and to protect world heritage from the claws of destruction and war.

Some people might say it is a bit of a "luxury" to mourn the loss of books and manuscripts when there is so much human suffering in the world. But I believe they are inextricably related – the suffering of humans, the tragedy of wars, civil wars, genocides and the deliberate destruction of culture, the burning of libraries.

When you demolish a library you are destroying memory.

Erasing the stories of who we are and who we were and who we can be.

In one of my earlier novels, *The Architect's Apprentice,* I wrote about the fate of a scientific library in Istanbul in the sixteenth century. Back then a brilliant Arab scientist, an eminent scholar of mathematics and clocks, had come to Istanbul, whereupon he would become the chief astronomer to the palace. His name was Taqi ad-Din. With his initiative the Sultan agreed to build a great astronomical observatory in the hills of the capital. From now on Taqi ad-Din and his fellow colleagues could observe the skies, unravel the secrets of constellations and stars. Inside the observatory they also put up a fascinating library, bringing in precious collections from both East and West. It wouldn't last long though. The religious fanatics began to grumble and loudly complain. They said it was a sin for human beings to turn their eyes toward the firmament when God was looking down at humans from up there. They said science was a sin. In 1580 the observatory was razed to the ground by Ottoman navy artillery, the library completely demolished. The cultural and scientific accumulation of centuries was wrecked in a matter of hours. It wasn't the first time, and it wouldn't be the last time, fanatics targeted culture and science.

Around the same time the king of Denmark was building a spectacular observatory for Tycho Brahe. Unlike its counterpart in the Ottoman Empire, this observatory would live and thrive, and make enormous contributions to knowledge by paving the way for Kepler's discoveries on the orbits of planets.

The age we are living in has been repeatedly baptized as "The Age of Information." Other denominations have also been used, such as "Computer Era," "New Media Era," or "Bitcoin Era." But in truth, it often feels to me that we have entered "The Age of Angst." Individual, collective and global anxiety has reached unprecedented levels. There is growing uncertainty, anger, frustration, disillusionment. Paradoxically, at a time when we were all supposed to find a voice thanks to the proliferation of digital technologies, so many of us feel voiceless.

East and West, wherever we might be, we all struggle with negative emotions, day in, day out. How then might one find traces of optimism, pockets of hope? Where to turn our attention, what to focus on? I believe wherever in the world you see a new library being built, or libraries being supported, that is exactly where hope resides.

A public library is a democratic space. In fact, public libraries are among our last remaining democratic spaces.

Today knowledge is under attack like never before. Societies have become bitterly polarized, divided into epistemological tribes that obtain their information from "alternative" sources. There is a deeply anti-intellectual strand inherent to populist nationalism and populist authoritarianism that often goes unnoticed but is highly destructive and dangerous. The animosity against intellect and intellectuals is an alarming sign. While nativism, extremism and conspiracy theories all keep attacking science and truth, libraries are bravely celebrating learning, wisdom, diversity and inclusion. The doors of a library, just like the doors of a storybook, are open to everyone – regardless of race, ethnicity, gender, religion or class. When we enter a library, the first thing we do is to drop our voices – we become a bit more humble, a bit more willing and ready to listen to others, we leave our egos outside.

Every study conducted in the last years has shown that there is a sharp decline in public trust in politics, politicians, even some of the oldest social institutions. It is remarkable that libraries are still symbols of public trust. In 2016 a PEW research study found out that more than 78 percent of adults in the USA regard "libraries as guiding them to information that is trustworthy and reliable." This figure is even higher among millennials. At a time of extreme divisions, libraries are spaces of coexistence.

As I am writing this piece it has been announced in the UK that there will be severe budget cuts affecting arts and culture. Libraries have always suffered from austerity, cultural centers have been the first places to be shut down at times of economic uncertainty. Many politicians do not seem to understand that we need books just like we need water and air. They do not seem to understand that dissolving libraries has far-reaching social, cultural and political consequences. A society that does not invest in culture is more prone to conflict, antagonism, division, clash and tension.

Kudos, then, to the city and the people of Oslo. Deichman Bjørvika, with its unusual architecture and warm and welcoming inner space, has already become a cultural, social and intellectual hub, an extraordinary place where minds and hearts meet, knowledge is gently nourished and learning is openly encouraged.

A library is more than a mere collection of books. It is an act of secular faith.

Faith in humanity and its ability to improve as a species.

That is what this beautiful library in Oslo symbolizes for me: hope, resilience, resistance, courage and ultimately, faith in a better world.

Public Libraries – A Triumphant Story or Desolation Headed for the Scrapyard of History?

Liv Sæteren

Being more interested in libraries than your average person, I visit the library whenever I find myself in a new place. A visit to the library – whether at home or abroad – can roughly result in one of two experiences.

Some libraries are teeming with life, filled with people in activity or at leisure, conversing, studying. The place has is a vibrant pulse and warmth. Colors, furniture calling out to be used, exhibitions…

In other libraries time has ground to a halt: rows of monotonous bookcases filled with orderly arranged tomes, reading sections with solid, plain chairs and tables. Maybe some colorful children's furniture in one area, and if I look closely, I might find traces of recent technological innovation in the form of computers on desks. The tristesse is not dissipated by the presence of designated rooms for events and meetings, and it can permeate small venues just as easily as pompous, monumental buildings. These places are silent and more or less empty.

Two parallel library universes containing more or less the same elements: books, tables, chairs, computers, staff. Why such differences?

The life and pulse of a library is more than a function of the building and interior decoration. It also depends on what kind of content you encounter in the shelves, which objects are exhibited, the competence, energy and presence of the staff, and the range of programs and activities on offer. But there's no denying that your visual intake – spaces, shapes, colors – is what forms your first impression of the place. A library ought to be a space for sharing all the stories of the world. But an uninteresting space says that this place is … uninteresting! By that I mean to say that architecture and interior design make a real difference.

The project "Library Ranking Europe" ranks libraries on a star scale from 1 to 6. Two former library directors visit European libraries in situ and assess their physical appearance, visible activities and online presentation. Only a handful get 6 stars. A first impression is not easily changed …

A Backwards Glance – Storytelling

The most important revolution in library practices in Europe and particularly in the Nordic countries occurred around the turn of the nineteenth century.

Prior to that, library collections were mostly in storage rooms. Librarians would fetch out their treasures on request, either for home loans or to be perused on location.

The spatial typology of libraries stems from that combination of storage rooms and systematically ordered bookcases, a desk for transactions between staff and customer and study halls designed for quiet reading.

The Modern Public Library

We like to ascribe library development in the Nordic countries and parts of Europe to Deichman. When Haakon Nyhus was appointed chief librarian of Oslo in 1898, he imported some innovative ideas from the United States. Public libraries belonged to the PEOPLE, bookcases were to be taken out of secluded storage rooms and placed where people could amble around and LOOK and choose for themselves. He also found ways to bring books out to where the people were – in parks, on tramways…

Nyhus's ideas gained prominence, establishing the modern public library and a Nordic thinking around libraries: democratic access to sources of knowledge and culture for all citizens. And delegations arrived from far and near to learn.

Stagnation in Norway

Construction work on Oslo's new main library commenced in 1922, and the building was completed in 1933. However, the jewel in Nyhuus's crown was as heavy as lead. Its architecture still resembled that of its forerunners, with their storage rooms and reading halls. A mere fifth of the area and collection were accessible to the audience. The building "monumentalized" the institution and its practice, and after that development slowed to a snail's pace, with an exception for new presentation methods for children and school collaboration.

Norwegian libraries outside the larger cities were terribly small and sparse. A meager national economy combined with thinly populated rural areas meant that Norwegian libraries remained backwards institutions compared to our neighboring countries.

The Library Shall Be Built upon Law

Norwegian libraries may have lacked resources in the pre- and post-war periods, but that does not mean they were low on ambition. The Nordic countries shared a common notion of libraries as instrumental in giving everyone equal access to knowledge. In 1971 a new Library Law kicked new life into the Norwegian public libraries. Numerous tiny, isolated and independent book collections housed in miserable locations with short opening hours and part-time staff were to be transformed into a unified library system in each municipality, with main libraries and branches – and qualified librarians.

Organizing and funding, norms, standards, minimum requirements and injunctions – these were the tools. Norms for book collections were introduced, for opening hours adapted to population numbers, for premises, for distance between bookcases etc.

In the seventies the profession became highly politicized – with lofty ambitions on behalf of the users. No matter where you lived, you could have any book forwarded to a library near you, mainly due to a national book-loaning collaboration and visions of "the Norwegian Library" as a national system, the principle of free services and egalitarian ideals regardless of geographical location.

Projects and Development?

It is quite a challenge to further development and change when raising standards to a minimum level is still a primary goal. In order to introduce new practices within a tight budget, you have to rearrange your priorities. Which is painful. However, some development and projects were being tested out, particularly in middle-size municipalities. Public information, marketing and new media such as music and video were added to the agenda. The authorities funding developmental work in libraries were primarily concerned with issues like library services to marginalized groups: disabled people, the blind or those with reduced eyesight, residents in institutions, prison inmates, immigrants and refugees. All important enough, but hardly any focus on the development of general library services.

Extended Culture Concept, Culture Services and Culture Centers

The time was simply not right for pumping large national resources into a sector so stuck in the past. The seventies saw extensive reformations of public services: a transfer of power from government to local county or municipal authorities. At the same time parliament reports started to extend the concept of culture, placing emphasis on activities outside of cultural institutions – such as individual projects and hobbies. Culture councils and administrations appeared, and libraries tended to end up at several removes from the local council's political organs.

The era of parliament reports was also the era of culture centers. State incentives led to the establishment of culture centers in many municipalities, fully equipped with theater stages and concert halls, meeting rooms, vestibules and cafés. But they were often more or less empty, as they lacked an organization to direct them. Meanwhile libraries were struggling in cramped premises with no room for meetings or group sessions, and bookcases on wheels that were hauled out whenever a school class or kindergarten visited.

But Do We Even Need Libraries?

The rapid growth of information technology led politicians to pose questions: What will the practical use of libraries be when any information can be contained in a gadget the size of a sugar cube? In some cases, the cemented idea that libraries means *book* loans led to political rejection of introducing new media into libraries, and in other cases to decisions to rent out videos and music, even though the Copyright Act prohibits rental of a third party's intellectual or creative work.

Information Technology and New Development

Meanwhile, information technology was in continual development, and the libraries were in the forefront when it came to using computers. Library services are to a large extent about logistics, and computer programs were developed to alleviate time-consuming routines like cataloguing, searching, loans and returns.

Automation of routines led to a change in work tasks for librarians and, in principle, freed more time for customer contact. Freed time easily turns into more time spent on what you are already doing... Analyses of goals, tools and strategic ideas were overdue.

The Library World

If the start of the twentieth century signaled a major shift in public library practices, particularly in the Nordic countries, the closing of the twentieth century heralded a new era for libraries – all around the world.

A common heading for library meetings in the eighties and nineties was "Libraries in the Information Age." One could argue that library communities and politicians were stuck in their ancient ideas about library services. In public statistics, a library's most important measure of success was its book loan statistics. The utility value of that in an approaching "Information Age" was questionable.

Since the mid-eighties I have had the privilege of following and participating in global library developments – through the close collaboration of Nordic capital city libraries as well as through The International Federation of Library Associations (IFLA) and its section for Metropolitan Libraries.

Seen from that vantage point, the Nordic countries were at the vanguard of Europe. Finland and Denmark were especially resourceful. Norway, however, was like a poor cousin and lagged far behind. The Helsinki and Copenhagen libraries' budgets were twice the size of Oslo's, Stockholm's was about 40 % higher and even Reykjavik had a budget that was 15 % higher than Oslo. Even so, they all shared the same uncertainty with regard to technological developments, threats of budget cuts, and organizations that were low on experience and drive when it came to implementing changes. Elsewhere in Europe the situation was rather bleak – except for The Netherlands, where they had invested in several new libraries.

Outside of Europe the United States and Canada stood out in making significant investments in the library sector. Libraries often played a main part in local councils' educational projects for marginalized groups. There were many impressive integrational programs for new citizens from different cultural backgrounds. This was a slightly different approach from the one taken in Scandinavia, where focus was more on the importance of staying in touch with one's own language and culture.

Outside of the Anglo-American library tradition, Singapore became the destination for many field trips and conferences. There, libraries were used to modernize education to satisfy the nation's need for competent users of information technology.

Headline themes at IFLA's annual world conferences around the turn of the century give one an idea of common focus areas like knowledge, education, information, technology and freedom of speech. Another recurring theme is reading and the battle against illiteracy.

It is important to remember the extreme differences between the "Anglo-Nordic" library world and library services in countries with widespread illiteracy, where librarians struggle to spread at least a few books with the scarce resources they have at their disposal. In places like that programs to teach and promote reading will be the central task for a long time to come.

A New Understanding of Libraries

Purpose and Public Duty

From a historical point of view, Norway and several other countries have had library laws that define libraries as part of their communities' infrastructure, with a clearly expressed goal: to promote enlightenment, education and culture. Traditionally, book loans have been their most important tool in that regard, with necessary additions and changes triggered by an ever changing media reality.

Norwegian library terminology used to cement the notion that libraries mainly existed to loan books: *boklånere* (*book lenders*) and *lånekort* (*lending cards*) instead of *users* and *library cards.* Therefore, a new terminology was required, as well a new understanding of a library's purpose and the new tools at its disposal.

Oslo's approach to this was to launch an extensive program of tests and development projects. A plethora of novelties appeared: philosophy cafés, "Book and baby"-events, knit and listen, language cafés, pop-up libraries at festivals, systematic training courses for teachers to promote reading in kindergartens, universities for the elderly, etc.

These were all modest changes, but they added up to what could be regarded as a paradigm change in the shape of a new understanding of the library as a cooperative institution that interacted with local environments, other institutions in various fields of specialization, and in its employment of new professional work groups.

New methods and services were introduced by identifying various user segments and tailoring presentation programs and marketing; by lifting up specific themes and hiring competence from outside the organization to help present them; by including volunteers and NGOs in presentation programs.

The path went from internally defined goals and services to involving the user as a resource in the development of services. This also meant saying goodbye to established professional ideals such as neutrality, objectivity and equal treatment.

The stereotypical image of the library as an institution for book loans was replaced by a new understanding of its public function as a provider of spaces that bring together published content and people.

The Public Library as Social Actor

In the nineties, public libraries were among the first public institutions to offer Internet access as a service. Libraries provided their users with search desks and offered training in how to use the Internet and information technology and thus became a more interesting social actor in the eyes of government, NGOs and users alike. When libraries lacked know-how or capacity, they teamed up with other professional environments.

By now, an increase in the number of citizens with foreign background was growing into a major challenge for society. Again, libraries stepped up to play an important role. Immigrant communities tended not to be active users of public services in general, but libraries quickly became an exception.

Step by step, the libraries were becoming a modern social actor and coordinator, working with volunteers and NGOs and drawing on a wide array of competencies to achieve important social goals.

Presentation – From Neutrality to Temperature

The "novelty" in how libraries activated knowledge and inspiration sources lies in how they abandoned their fundamental principles of objectivity and neutrality, that is, their commitment to an average standard for content and services.

Neutrality tends to make presentations lukewarm and uninspiring. When you decide to make a presentation, you are already deciding to forefront something at the expense of something else, and you are addressing a certain segment of users to the exclusion of others. The sum of differences can still amount to a good and wide totality...

Public Discussion and Meeting Places

The new narrative of libraries used multiple terms to express their new function: meeting place, arena, communal hall, square, the "third place" (as in the place between work or school and home).

A library that promotes societal engagement and participation by arranging public debates on local council plans or on controversial literature, exhibitions/programming courses, comic strip workshops and so forth, becomes a place where people meet and exchange ideas and opinions. Unfortunately, many libraries are still poorly equipped for those kinds of activities. In 2007 the first House of Literature was opened in Oslo, to be followed by others all over the nation. Their function is basically to arrange the kind of activities libraries already engage in or *ought* to engage in.

However, Houses of Literature were launched as a unique "brand," as libraries' activities in the same field were relatively invisible and "prosaic." This has probably spurred libraries to intensify and highlight their literary events and debates, and contributed to the inclusion of a paragraph in the Norwegian Library Law of 2013 stating that public libraries are independent meeting spaces and arenas for public discussion and debate.

Are There Limits to What a Library Can Do?

Innumerable new methods can be employed to engender interest in new information, to help people acquire knowledge and manage their lives.

Maker space in the digital field is a natural development of the library's mission to increase the public's knowledge of, and mastering of, information technology. Open-for-all workshops with other forms of technical equipment ay be seen as a natural continuation.

Services like seed libraries and loaning arrangements for tools and sports equipment can be viewed as efforts to increase public interest in environmental issues or part of a local strategy to encourage sharing. Help to understand official documents and forms, and active presentations of municipal information lie within the library's tasks and competence. In some places there are plans to maybe extend this in the form of "citizen services" – a kind of guidance through bureaucratic mazes.

When a municipality or local council wants to introduce a new service, they will naturally try to place it within the library institution, as it already has established opening hours, a staff that are used to handling units, are service-minded and deal with a wide user base. The library sector must discuss its priorities and decide which services lie within its public mandate and which should be placed elsewhere, no matter how pleasant or useful they might be.

Opening Hours – Around-the-Clock/Extended Hours

The most recent and radical trend is the extension of opening hours, in other words allowing the public access to the library outside the working hours of the staff. Admission cards with pin codes, surveillance cameras and security guards are integral elements here. The authorities place a lot of trust in their citizens when they offer them a meeting place for learning, fun and work without demanding more than civil conduct in return. It is food for thought that wage costs can be converted into security staff and "cleaning" at the expense of employees committed to presentation and sharing of information.

Considering the many available tools and beneficial services that logically could be delegated to a modern library, there is one issue that always crops up, and that is that the spaces have to be designed along entirely different guidelines than the present typology.

Library Buildings and Architecture

How are you invited into a house or space? What is your first impression? How quickly do you see what you seek? Do you see other offers you might avail yourself of in addition to your original errand?

When library staff see bookcases lined with books ordered by alphabet or decimal classification, they see an ocean of knowledge and possibilities, a key to understanding, reading ability and insight, excitement and adventure.

Not everybody may see it that way. Someone who enters a library for the first time in order to borrow a novel will mainly see fiction in the bookcases next time she comes, too.

Commissioning a Library

150 years ago, a library space was a rather easy order – square meters, bookcases, chairs and tables, desks. All over the world many beautiful libraries have been created along those lines; magnificent, monumental, architecturally prestigious structures – iconic buildings on a par with churches, theaters, museums... Iconic buildings set an example and establish a standard for similar structures for many decades – perhaps centuries – to come.

Modern spatial programs also set quantitative requirements for seating and workspaces for users and employees, square meters and shelf space for various media and spaces for different types of events.

If a commission limits itself to those kinds of specifications, architects and other involved parties in public building projects will look to past examples. Their ambition will be to create a unique architectonic expression, but within the limits of an established typology.

When library buildings have to be drastically changed because the media landscape and working methods have changed, the library as client and the architects must embark on a creative process and create a new typology together.

Collaboration between the Library as User and the Architect

Local government and casework in building matters are a formidable challenge when it comes to developing optimal library buildings and interiors.

A traditional local council approach to planning might be: Technical questions sort under the technical departments. User participation (from library staff who will be running the business, and customers) "is expensive, users always want more and more, which is why building matters should be decided and run by technical departments, law/financing and politicians."

When it comes to monumental or prestigious buildings, their grading in a hierarchy will probably also mean something in the struggle for attention from the powers that be. This means that there are many reasons why library managements are denied much formal status in building matters and are shut out of any dialogue with the architects.

If library managements were allowed to set more conditions, would that guarantee success? Not necessarily. The library community's interest and competence with regard to premises – apart from size and location – has been rather modest. There is a lack of awareness when it comes to the importance of interior architecture and the scale of spatial and interior changes present and future library services will have to face. But things are changing. Not least in the process around Oslo's new main library, which has heightened our awareness of the instrumental value of library space.

What Manner of Formal and Spatial Changes? A New Library Typology!

I would go so far as to say that we initiated conceptual development of a new type of library when we in 1992 proposed the idea of moving the main library from an inefficient, high-maintenance monumental building to a failed shopping mall. The concept was launched under the slogan "library of the future," with differently furnished and designed rooms that gave users a clear overview of the library's wide variety of services, and where different user groups could feel at home and at ease. This notion sparked enthusiastic political resolutions to give the main library a new, forward-looking venue.

The essential feature of the concept is that the library's content and services are incredibly varied and diverse, as are the users and their needs and behaviors. Therefore, a library's spaces and interiors need to play an active role in supporting and conveying its content.

The concept was refined over a number of years and a number of alternative locations and buildings (more than 20 alternatives and two architecture competitions). It was shared and discussed in meetings and international conferences, and several new libraries in Norway and Europe were realized before the first stone of Oslo's new main library was laid down.

Things take time, for better or worse. As we waited for the library to become a reality, experiences from other branches that were being refurnished and upgraded – often with impressive results – helped us refine and develop our concept.

Oslo's New Main Library

The building that now stands ready in Bjørvika is the result of a process that has taken almost thirty years. The old main library checked off on all the hackneyed phrases of "book temple" and "citadel of learning," with stairs and architectural features that, at best, sent signals of solemn loftiness or, at worst, rejection.

The architectural style of Deichman Bjørvika, on the other hand, draws you in and gives you an immediate impression of all its floors. You see that the building contains a multitude of stories and narratives. It has an open appearance, yet with diversions and side paths that offer surprises as well as secluded spaces for reflection. Practically all areas of the building are accessible to the users. Large, yes, monumental, yes, but generously open, with inward and outward views.

The building was planned in collaboration with the library organization as a distinct and creative voice, with a wide-ranging staff owning the project and fighting both alongside and against top-notch architects in a creative dialogue. The building communicates that there is plenty to discover and experience here, and that you will be continually surprised. But there is one fly in the ointment: Large areas of the ground floor have been leased to commercial interests. That is shameful.

The Effect of a New Type of Library Space

Wherever one has invested in new buildings with attractive interiors and a variety of programs and services, the effect has been considerable. Users flock to the library and spend more time there. There is a growing understanding of how libraries can be efficient tools in small- and large-scale town development.

The numbers are unequivocal: redesigned library branches in Oslo have led to two or three times as much usage, as well as increases in book loans. Similar results have been reported from all other places that have invested in attractive premises offering a variety of activities. A new downtown library in Helsinki has been a staggering success, with 3.1 million visitors the year it opened.

Interiors as Presentation Tools

New interiors provide results. Until now, focus has mainly been on the attraction factor. Inviting buildings and spaces designed with an eye for the preferences of a variety of user groups. The next point on the agenda should be how we can shape spaces as tools for content presentation. That implies a focus on exhibition architecture and scenography in addition to interior architecture. A library that aims to stage meetings between content and users needs to include scenography in its thinking around how to design spaces.

Presentation of Digitally Published Content

Books are still being published in great numbers, but we see a future where publications in many subject areas mainly will be digital. For libraries to fulfill their public duty, important digital information will also need a visual presence alongside printed and analog publications. That will require know-how, but equally important: interiors spatially suited to curating, displaying and conveying digital sources. As of now they are still invisible in library spaces – screens and digital surfaces tend to contain information about the programs and services the library offers or provide additional information about books in their collection. Even the newest, most modern libraries treat digital tools and equipment as something separate from the "content" of the library, which primarily consists of physical objects. Access to digital resources is normally limited to search functions the users can operate themselves. Digital services and tools are usually situated in designated zones or rooms. Exhibitions and events also tend to be held in separate rooms or zones.

Future developers should seek new spatial solutions where physical and digital sources are integrated with tools, exhibition surfaces and interiors that are suited for presentations, activities and interactivity. Hopefully, the new Deichman main library will be a motor for innovation and further development in this field.

Success or Scrapyard?

Even poorly funded, dull libraries have a program for children and visiting school classes. Libraries are doing their very best. But in the twenty-first century the world comes pouring in through our phones, and our sphere of concentration is under attack around the clock. A library consisting of rows of gray bookcases and grayish-brown chairs and desks is not first on our list of go-to places for work, study or sleep. I do not see a very bright future for library systems like that. And there are plenty of those kinds of libraries around the world.

But although desolation still reigns in many places, the twenty-first century bears promise of change. Success breeds success – the stories of successful new libraries have created waves. New buildings are rising, and old ones are redesigned to become important elements in town planning, democratic development and the amassment of knowledge.

The successful innovative work that went into the planning of Oslo's new main library, combined with investment in new branches, has led to innovation in the whole library sector.

The Deichman-system has become one of the foremost in the world when it comes to innovations in methods and presentation spaces. There is reason to believe that this will lead to a lasting change in how we build new libraries and improve existing ones. The influx of people to the new main library on Oslo's seafront has made it clear what a library means for the inhabitants' quality of life. It's a new library story.

The main room of the old Deichman library
at Hammersborg (2000).

Introduction

This part of the book aims to give the reader insight into the project, as well as the process that led to the design and building of Deichman Bjørvika. We start with the competition and its ambitions for a new library, and show how the site relates to its nearest surroundings. Then we move on to our primary thoughts and analyses, sketches and trials, and further on through the project's development and the establishment of a multidisciplinary project group, via our meetings with manufacturers and contractors, the actual building process and all the way forwards to when the building was finished and finally could open its doors.

In addition to documentation of the finished building in drawings and photographs, we have included earlier sketches and model images to show how we, and many other architects, develop our projects. Architecture is a slow process, where abstract ideas and various suggestions are changed and reworked again and again before the project culminates in a physical building.

The content is more or less in chronological order, arranged by a few topics we consider to be the most important in order to grasp the library.

the Vestbanen site, which they had sold to the municipality a few years earlier, to make room for the new National Museum. Deichman would instead be located to Bjørvika. Five years of planning had to be cancelled. All the years of planning a new main library had nevertheless not been totally wasted. Through these processes, Deichman's ideas about a modern Nordic public library were developed and matured, and that would later form the basis for the planning of the new main library in Bjørvika.

This drawing was printed in the newspapers right after the opening of the library at Hammersborg and illustrates how the library was perceived as inaccessible due to the many stairs. For the new library, the librarians wanted a building free of thresholds and with good contact to the surrounding city.

The main room of the old Deichman library at Hammersborg (2000).

Bjørvika is the largest development area in Fjordbyen, the urban development project that opens the city toward the fjord by transforming infrastructure areas for future-oriented urban development with housing, recreation, and commercial areas. The new Opera House opened in 2008 and became the major generator for further development. In 2010, the highway was laid in a tunnel under Bispevika, and large areas of infrastructure were liberated. Highways and traffic machines that had created barriers between the city and the fjord could finally be transformed into a new, vibrant district.

Map of Bjørvika from 1917.

Image from the construction of the new Opera House in Bjørvika.

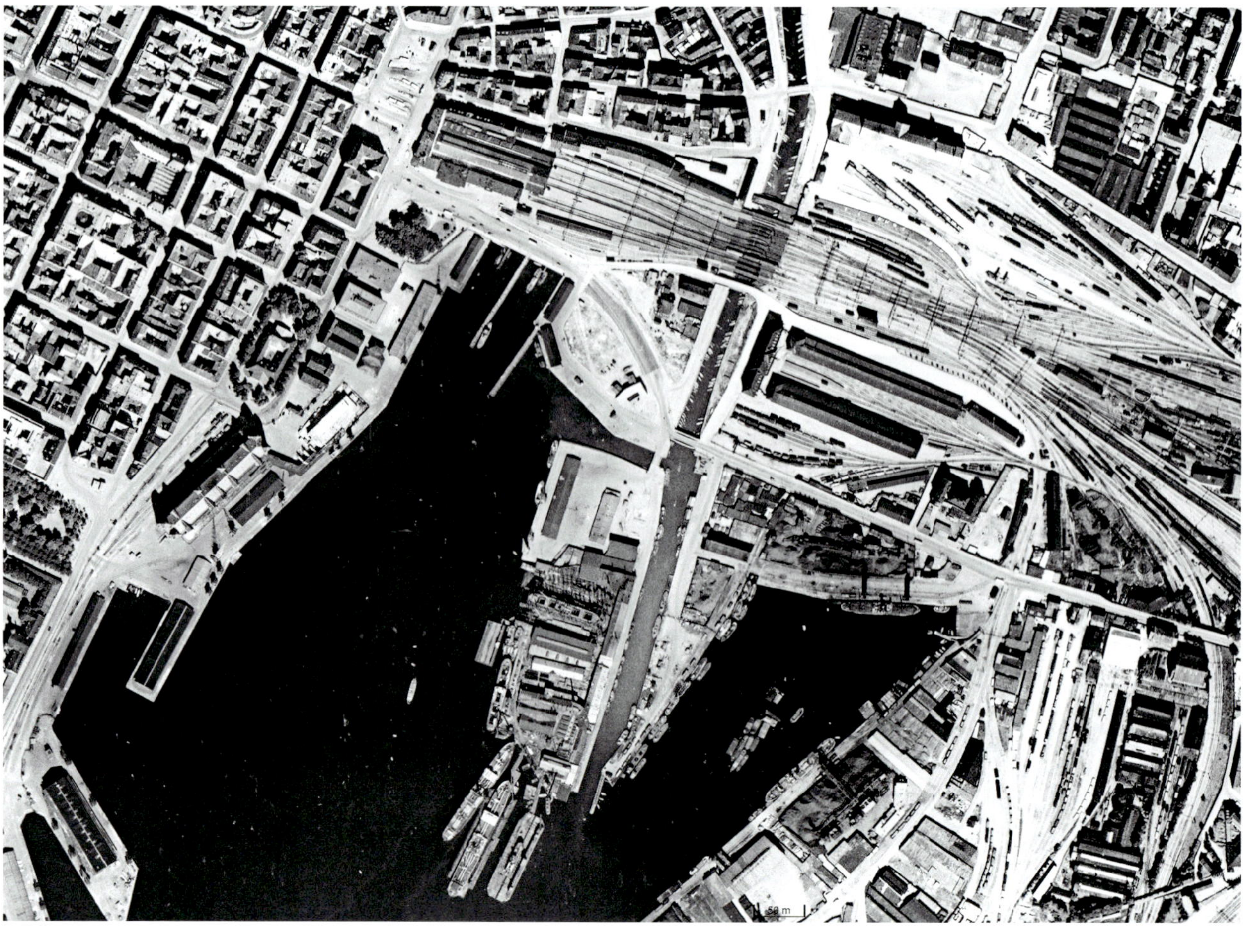

Historical image of Bjørvika. Before the highway was built, the area was characterized by port activities.

2 A Concept for the Library of the Future – The Architectural Competition

In 2008 a new competition for the main library was announced in parallel with the competition for a new Munch Museum. Both projects were to be neighbors of the newly opened Opera building. 10 international architectural firms were invited to the competition for the library, and 10 firms were selected through prequalification. The two architect firms Lundhagem and Atelier Oslo had had already collaborated on several projects, and together with the landscape architects Agence TER, we applied for prequalification. The competition program was conceptual and ambitious: What exactly is the library of the future, what building typology could accommodate this? The library had to be connected to the city and offer a space designed for people, not just for books.

The new building should be structured based on the users' need for services rather than on the collection, and should challenge traditional perceptions of how a library functions. The new library should to a lesser extent be organized around the storage and distribution of physical media. (excerpt from the competition program)

The librarians wanted to move away from the traditional "quiet" library, which was often dominated by rows of bookshelves.

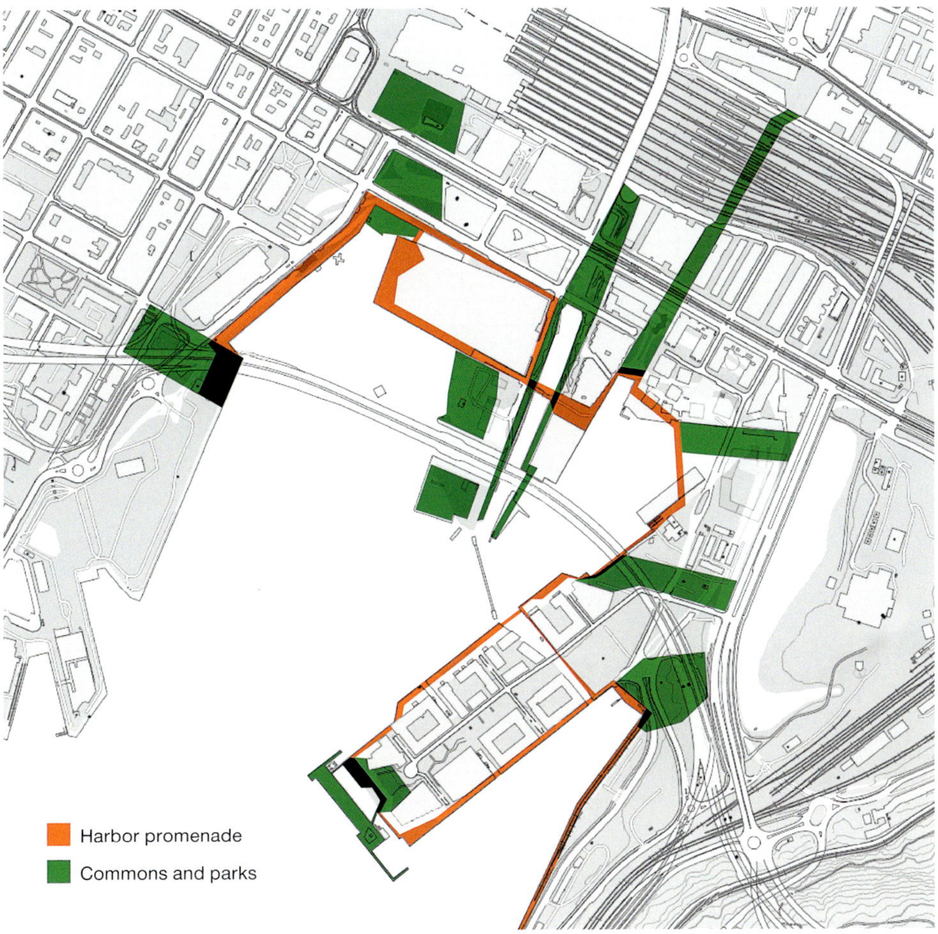

Plan of the 7 "commons" in Bjørvika. These public spaces structure the city plan for Bjørvika and were developed after a competition won by SLA and Gehl architects in 2004.

The competition was also not just about a new main library but in addition an urban development competition for the entire area on the north side of the Opera, called the "Deichman axis." The space requirement for the library filled only one-third of the total area. The participants were asked to propose functions for other buildings that could contribute to city life and create commercial value for the landowner, HAV Eiendom.

> 10 years of development, Bjørvika 2009 (top) and 2019 (bottom). The area for the "Deichman axis" is marked in red.

HAV Eiendom's objective is that the competition should show how a versatile and overlapping programming of urban functions can help to create a compact city on a human scale, which will downscale the current industrial character of the area. (from the competition program)

The competition area was divided into two plots by a planned road to the parking basement under the central station. A smaller plot, A8, faced west toward the Opera common, while a larger plot, A9, faced east toward the Akerselva River. The Opera, which was the nearest neighbor to the south, had already become a national icon. It was feared that the development in Bjørvika would shut off the Opera from the rest of the city, which led to a political decision to ensure the visibility of the Opera's entrance facade seen from the square in front of the central station, Jernbanetorget. The cut which that sight line made in the possible volume of the plot – in addition to the road dividing the area – put an important limitation on the design of the building and served as a central premise in the competition.

The area of the "Deichman axis" at the time the competition was announced. Several highway systems passed through the area, which was one of the main traffic routes in Oslo at the time. This created a major barrier between the city and the waterfront.

Plan and section of the sight line from the square in front of the central station to the Opera. From the competition program.

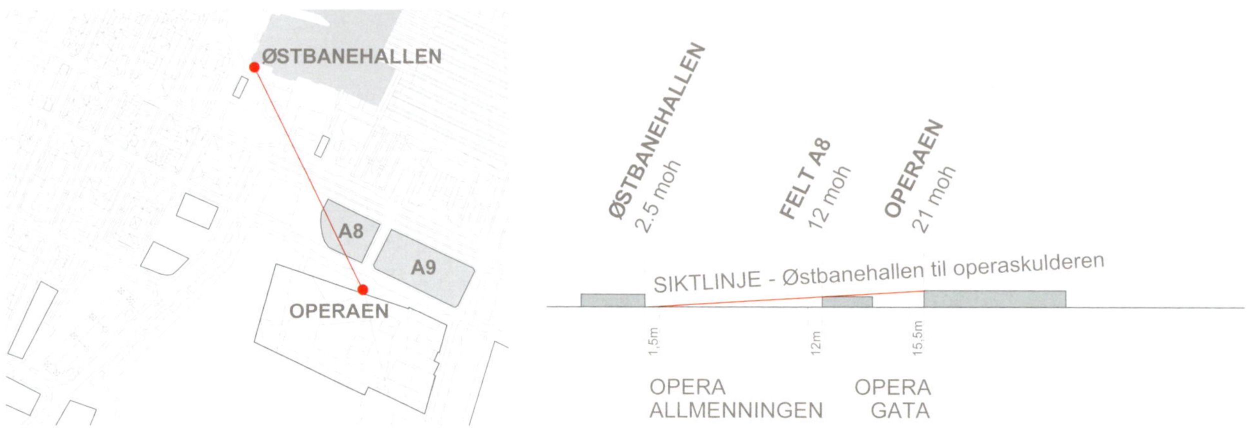

To Draw a Library

The competition program gave us to understand that librarians quite like the idea of serendipity, that is, unintentional discoveries. You might come to the library to look for a specific book but end up finding a different one from the one you had in mind, or you may instead discover an activity or event that raises your interest. We wanted to create a building that could facilitate these experiences: A space that would arouse the curiosity of the visitor and inspire a wandering. A building that could not be understood at first glance but had to be explored.

We tried to imagine life inside this building, which would contain multiple places with different scales and qualities. As inspiration and a common reference for the architect group through the process of developing the competition proposal, various themes were introduced such as lasting qualities, nature and the city.

Lasting qualities. The only thing we know for sure is that the library will be different in the future than it is today. Therefore, it was important to determine some lasting qualities that could leave other areas open to change, such as in a bazaar, where ancient constructions form a permanent background for ever changing life.

Nature. A space that changes as you move. Along the way, spaces of different character and quality arise. A continuous space that at the same time consists of several different places where you can sit. A room with different densities, where you sometimes come to a clearing and get an overview and can orient yourself. A space to explore. A space where you can find your own place. An open plain or a narrow shelf, where you can retreat. A building that is its own world.

Urbanity. A building like a small city. A library where you can find and explore unexpected opportunities and offers. An infrastructure that enables change. A place of energy and friction. Eventually, the project developed into a kind of vertical village, a continuous public space of squares and streets surrounded by smaller spaces, like small shops that present their goods to a passing audience.

It is important that the library is organized in a way that will allow the users to move in all directions in the building, and with a room distribution where open areas are combined with smaller, intimate zones. Public areas should have the best possible daylight conditions.
(from the competition program)

An imaginary information board was part of our submission. Here we tried to imagine life and activities on a normal day in the new library.

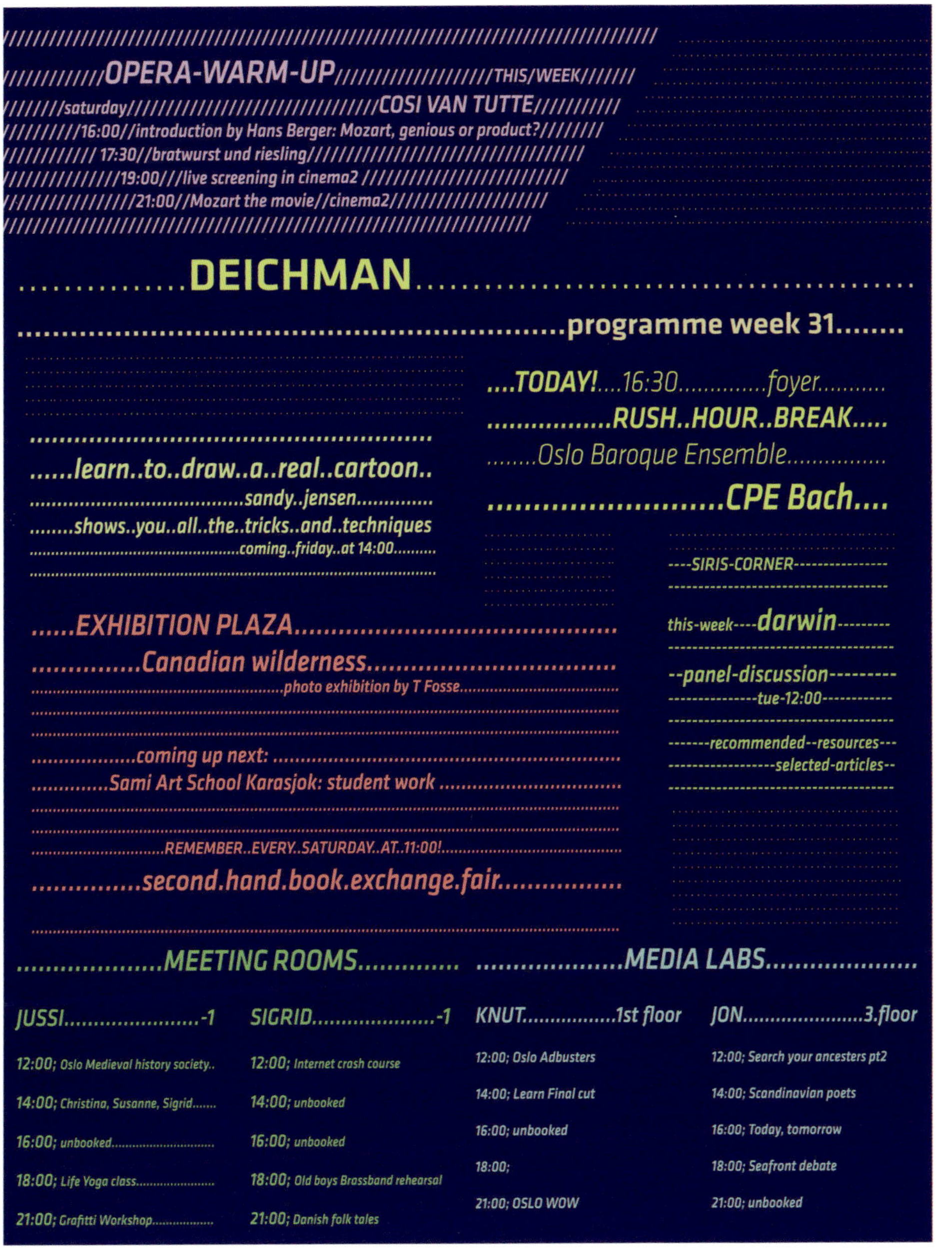

The Urban Structure

The competition area, which consisted of the two plots A8 and A9, forms an important urban connection between east and west, from the Opera common to the Akerselva River. It was to be planned for about 67,000 sqm gross area in total on the two plots, of which the library was to occupy about 20,000 sqm gross area.

There were mainly three alternative dispositions for how to place the library within the two plots that defined the competition area:

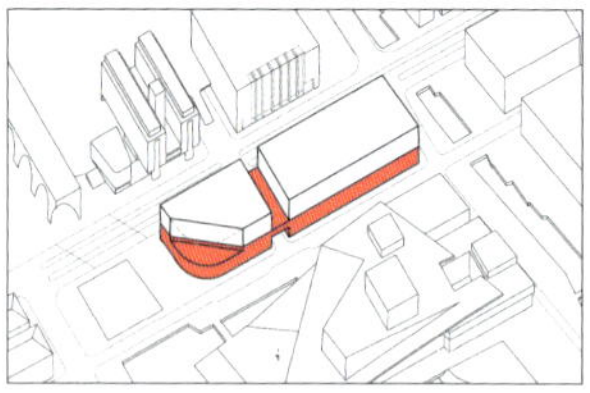

1 a horizontal library that spanned the entire area and had other functions/programs above it;

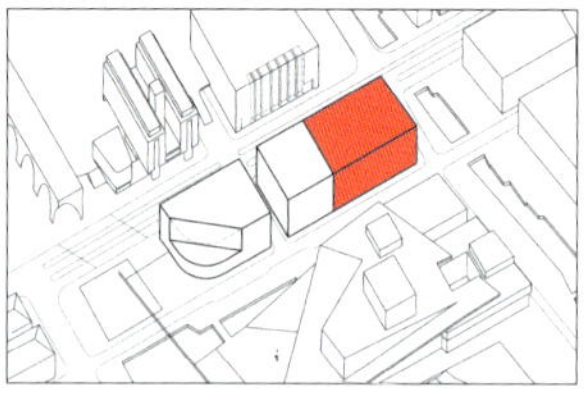

2 a vertical library facing east toward the Akerselva River;

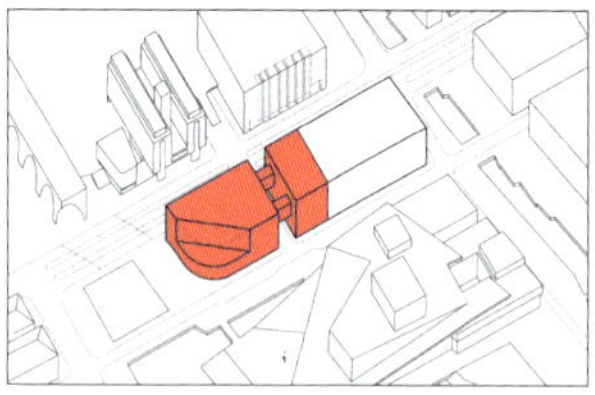

3 a vertical library facing west toward the Opera common.

Eventually we realized that a horizontal library would not fulfill the intentions we had developed for the library. A horizontal library would create long interior distances and not support the intention of serendipity, where visitors would be inspired to explore other parts of the collection and what they had to offer. A horizontal library over both plots, would create a monofunctional ground floor that would not contribute to a vibrant city life. Connecting the functions across the road between the two parts of the site would in practice also lead to a car tunnel running through middle of the project.

Instead of a large building that was dominated by one function on the ground floor, we wanted to divide the area into smaller buildings that could break down the scale, create intimate public spaces, interesting sight lines and walkways and weave into the urban fabric. With ground floors opening onto the street, we wanted to facilitate a varied urban life. To us, it seemed right that the library had to be a solitary building facing the Opera common to the west, even though the A8 site initially was too small for the space requirements of the library. The political decision to secure the sight line to the breakpoint at the Opera from Jernbanetorget (the public square in front of the central station) also resulted in a diagonal restriction for this plot that all competitors had to deal with.

Working models from the competition phase where different dispositions of the plots were examined. In the beginning, we studied many solutions for a horizontal library, since we thought that this would best respond to the desire for good contact with the city and the library. Eventually, however, we realized that this was wrong for both the library and the city. The solution was to divide the project into three volumes.

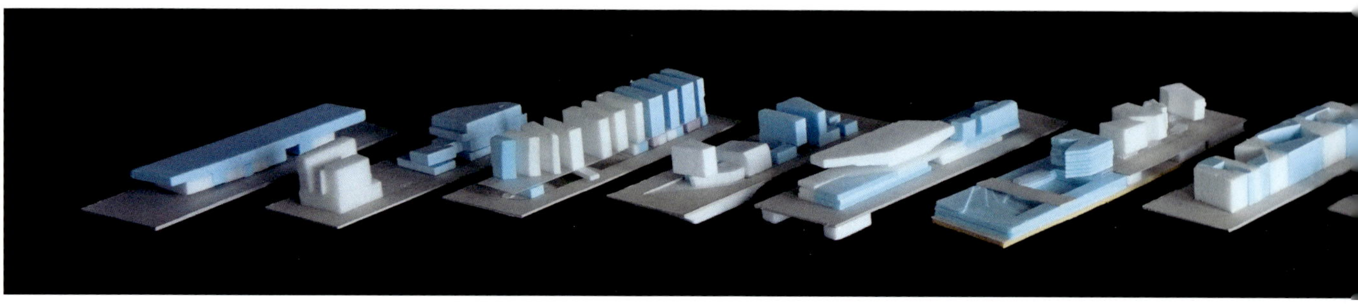

Our solution was to make a building with a shape based on cantilevers. By cantilevering over the sidewalk to the east and above the sight line of the Opera to the west, we created a building volume that was large enough to accommodate the library's space requirements. The cantilever to the west also gave the library a better orientation and visibility toward the city. The cantilever created a covered outdoor space which, along with the library's interior, could offer a protected public space, a good supplement to the attractive opera roof, where one is exposed to weather and wind.

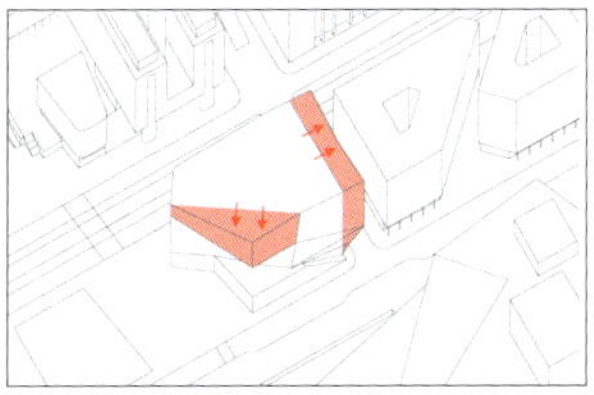

The cantilevers toward the Opera common and the street toward the east made it possible to bring the entire area required for the library inside the A8 plot.

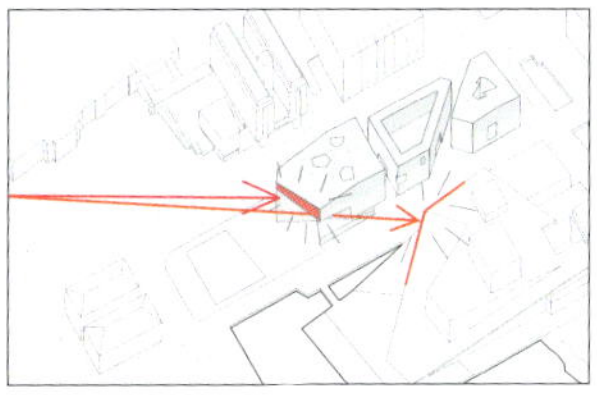

The cantilever also creates a clear front for the library toward the Opera common and advertises the library in the cityscape, at the same time as the relationship to the Opera and the sight line from Jernbanetorget was preserved.

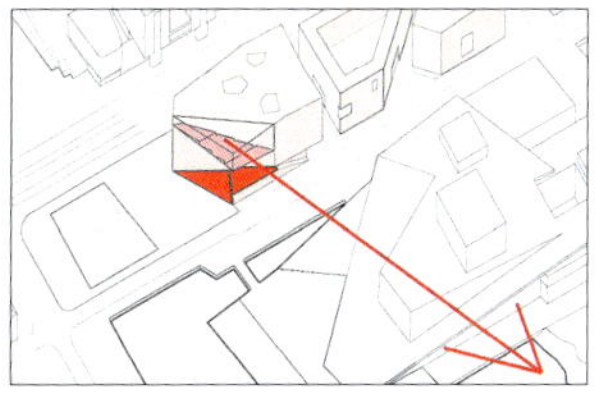

The cantilever creates a covered public space in front of the library at the same time as it creates a beautiful interior space with a view across the Opera to the fjord.

Illustration from the competition showing the library with the space in front.

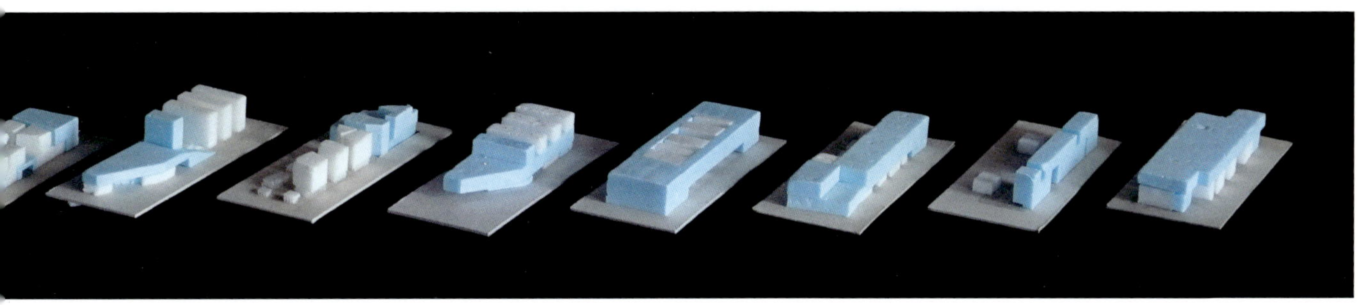

The other plot, A9, which faces the Akerselva River, we divided into two building volumes with a diagonal street opening a connection from the east to the front of the opera. This pedestrian street creates two smaller urban spaces that give life to the city. By dividing the "Deichman axis" into three solitary buildings, we wanted to connect the project to the urban fabric and facilitate city life on the ground floor, with active facades facing the street with small cafes, restaurants, and shops – in addition to the library itself.

The three buildings are connected underground with a basement and a docking area located under Robert Levins gate, which handles the library's logistics and distribution of media to other branches.

Since the library was located on the A8 plot with its main orientation to the west, the Opera common naturally became the library's front plaza. Here, we proposed to change the planned canal into a water mirror, in order to enlarge the space and allow for more varied use. The idea was a thin water mirror only a few cm deep that could be removed for larger events – or turned into an ice-skating rink in the winter. This idea was developed and adopted in 2012. SLA landscape architects were later given the responsibility of designing this space as part of the Opera common.

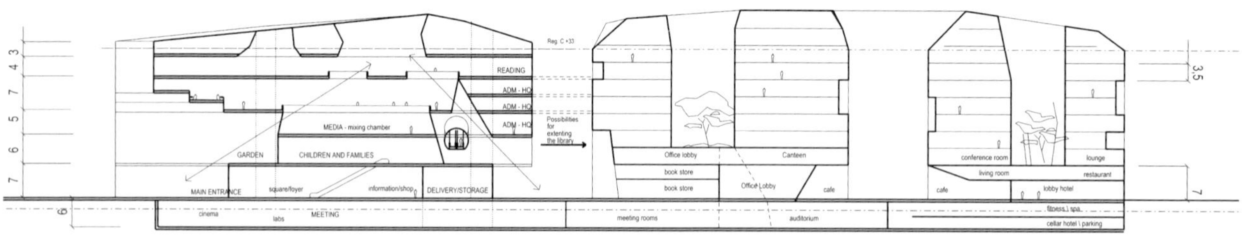

Section from the competition phase. The three buildings are connected by a common basement under both plots. Under the street dividing the two plots, there is a large docking area that can be reached via a ramp going through the student housing building on the A9 plot opposite the library. This is an important element for Deichman Bjørvika's role as a distributor of media to all the branches it has around Oslo.

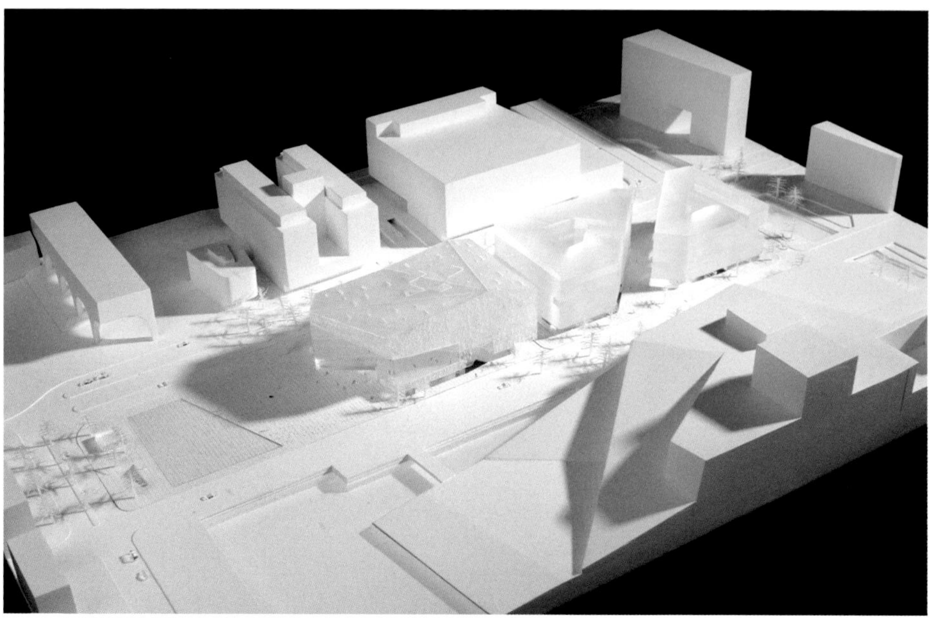

The competition model with the solitary library and the plot behind divided into two buildings.

The “Deichman axis” under construction. The diagonal division of the two buildings behind Deichman Bjørvika creates varied urban spaces.

Working models from the competition.

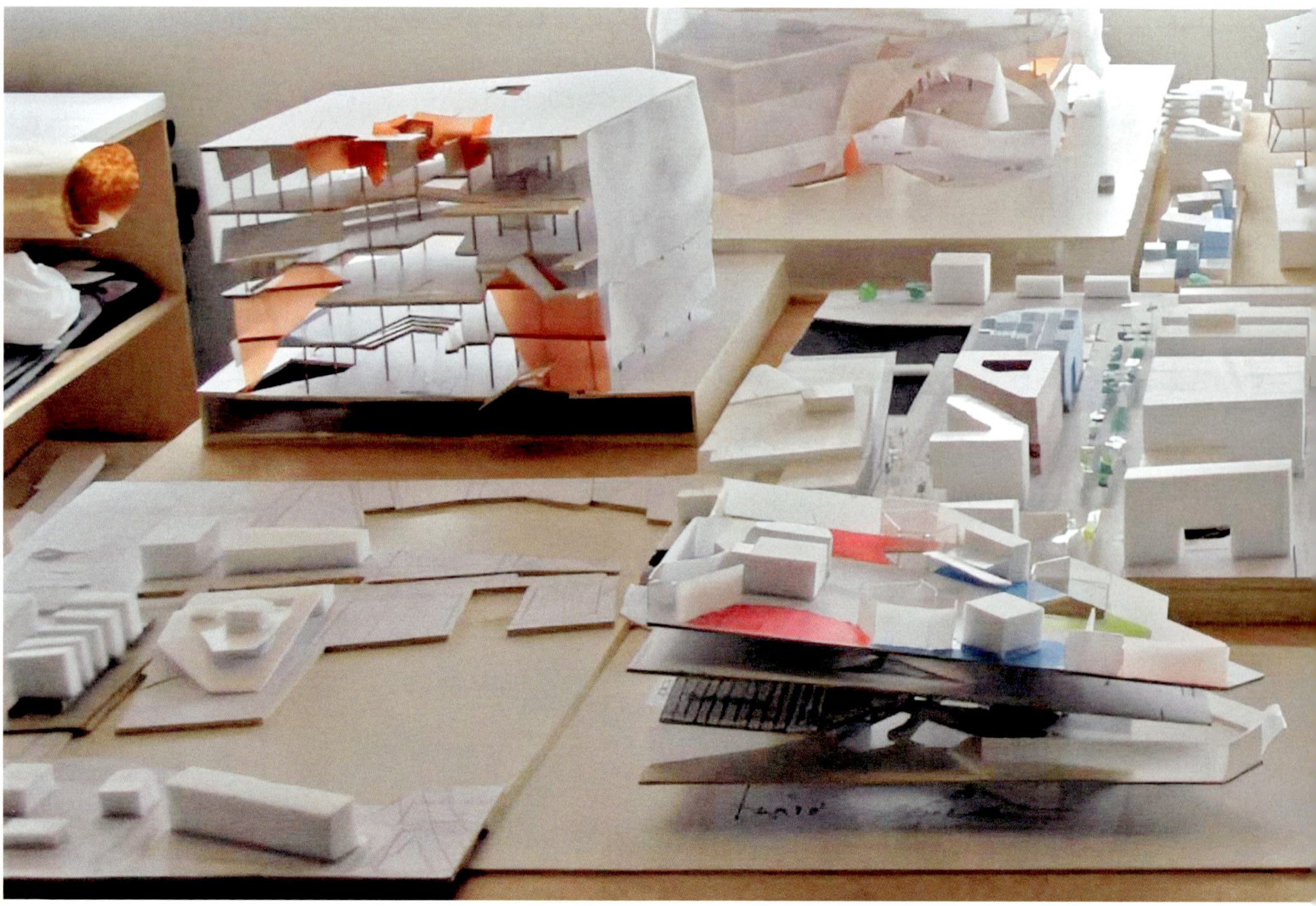

A Vertical Public Space

The limited footprint of the selected plot to the west resulted in a relatively compact and vertical building with five floors above ground. A main challenge was to connect these floors into a continuous public space with good daylight conditions in all areas.

Our overall ambition was to create a building that was both extroverted and introverted. We wanted a building with a clear connection to the public space in front and the surrounding streets, while at the same time offering a space for concentration and contemplation. A common solution to these concerns was the introduction of three diagonal atriums, light shafts that cut through the entire building. The light shafts connect the three entrances with three large skylights in the ceiling.

The three diagonal light shafts (four in the competition) intersect in the middle of the building and create a large interior space over several floors. The open library area is organized around this characteristic, light-filled space. The diagonal light shafts establish various connections between the library and the city, as well as between the different floors.

Thanks to the light shafts, we get a library that is extroverted toward the busy city outside, and at the same time becomes increasingly introverted

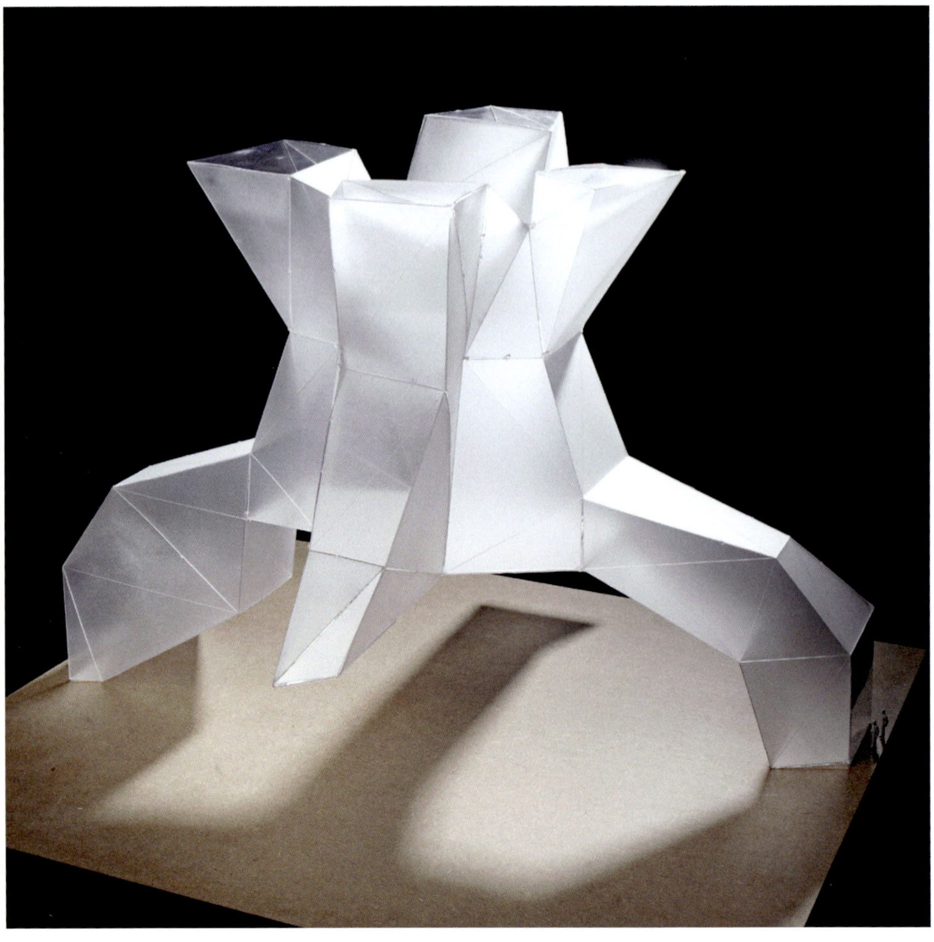

An abstract model of the interior space was submitted to the competition, instead of the detailed section model that was requested. The model helped to establish the light shafts as an important conceptual element that stayed put throughout the whole process.

and contemplative as you move upward in the building. The light shafts can be compared to a clearing in the forest and give every floor its unique design, since each level is cut through in different places. The library thus gets numerous intimate places within the large, continuous library space.

Although the Deichman Bjørvika has a complex and rich interior, the light shafts create a clear hierarchy that makes it easy to orientate.

The light shafts invite you to progress vertically through the building. Not everything is revealed at once, but you constantly discover new places and connections as you move.

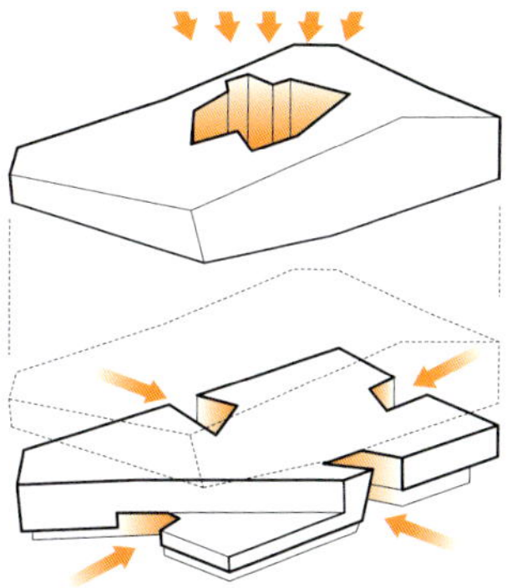

Diagrams from the competition. The light shafts create an interior that gradually changes from being extroverted on the lower floors to more introverted and contemplative higher up.

One of the main perspectives from the competition was from the interior, where you move upward in the light shafts toward the upper floors.

From an Active City Floor to a Place of Contemplation

We organized the program with the idea of achieving a natural flow of people and activities. In order to allow for a lot of activity on the lower floors without disturbing the calm and concentrated atmosphere at the top, the auditorium, cinema, and classrooms were located on the ground floor with easy access from the street. That would avoid dragging large crowds unnecessarily through the building. Areas for contemplation and concentration were located at the top, with the terraced area connecting the upper floors and overlooking the Oslo Fjord as the main attraction.

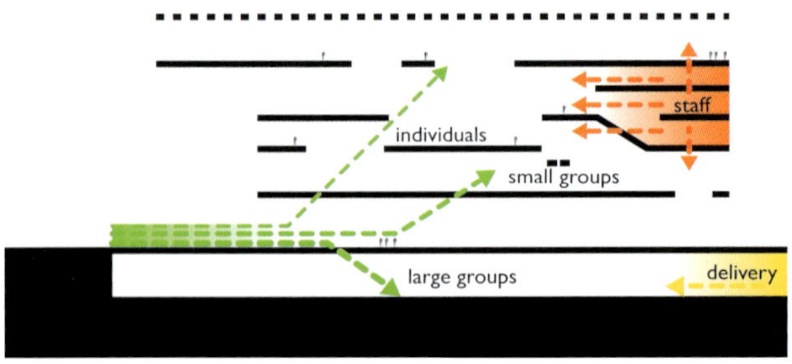

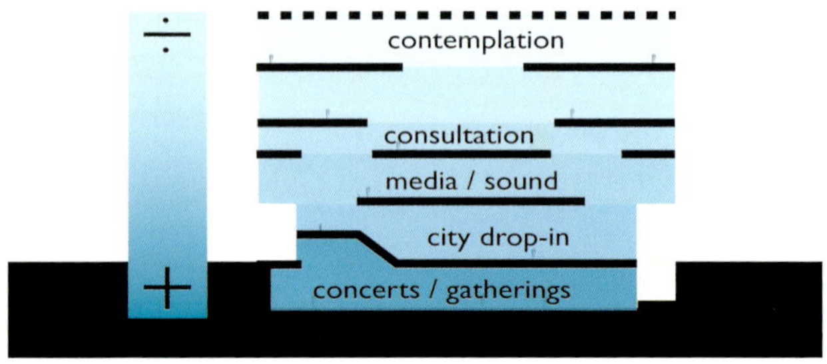

Diagrams from the competition. The vertical organization of the program and the flow of people created a transition from a busy urban square at the bottom to a place of contemplation at the top.

Study models and sketches that examine the connection between the various floor plans and program elements.

> Studies from the competition of the interior spaces created by the light shafts. The cycle of escalators was eventually placed into the light shafts to invite the user to move around the library and constantly offer new lines of sight and experiences.

Floor plan illustrations submitted for the competition. With a brief description of the thoughts behind the atmosphere and the program distribution on the various levels.

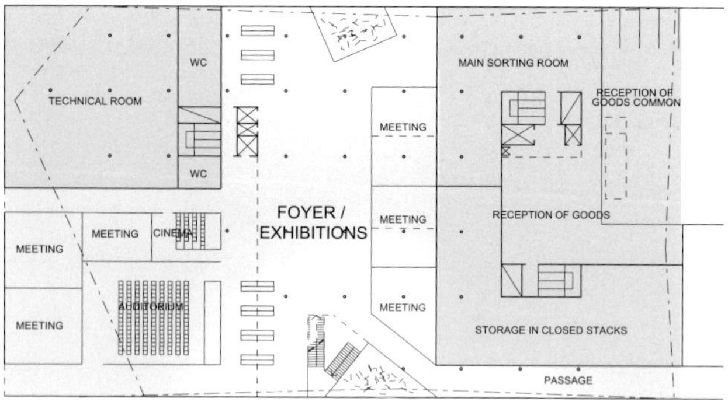

U1. Events / meetings The floor underground has big light shafts going down to a foyer with surrounding meeting and learning facilities. Here many events can happen at the same time without bringing large groups of people through calm zones of the library. There are optional connections to neighboring areas for cinema/concert/conference facilities. A large multifunctional hall for larger events can be placed under the plaza west of the Library.

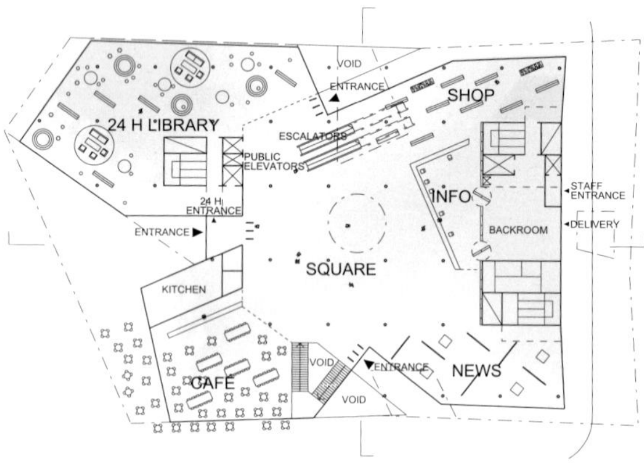

Street level The ground floor is the city drop-in level with entrances at the northeast, southeast, and west. Here you can easily upload your electronic book, lend from and return to the media collection, get quick guidance, shop media, have a coffee, read newspapers, or participate in a large gathering in the middle square.

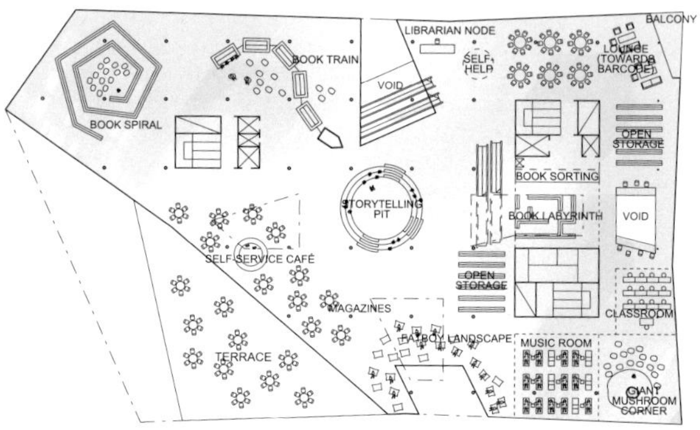

1. Multipurpose (media / sound) On the 1st floor we suggest multifunctional zones which can be arranged according to themes. More permanent zones for children and tweens can be placed here. Toward the south there is a beautiful terrace which can be linked to a magazine lounge and a music "bar."

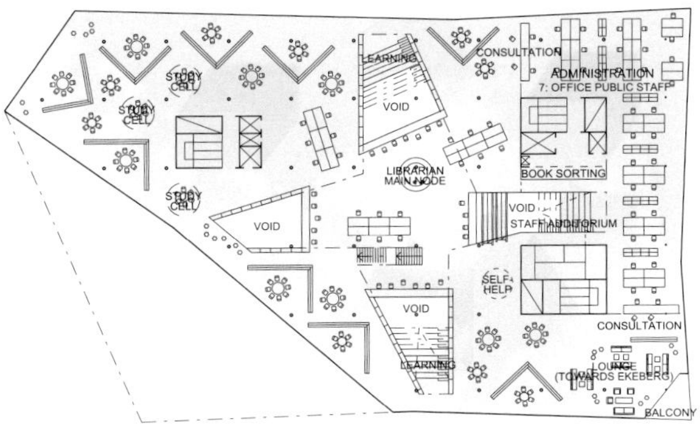

2. Main media / contemplation The 2nd floor is the entrance to the more silent atmosphere in the upper part of the building. The lifts and the escalator bring you directly up to the librarians' main node. Here are consultation tables which mix staff and public. On the same floor the librarians have back offices and meeting rooms. The light shafts give visual connection to the street life outside the building. An "oasis" brings the view toward Grefsenkollen.

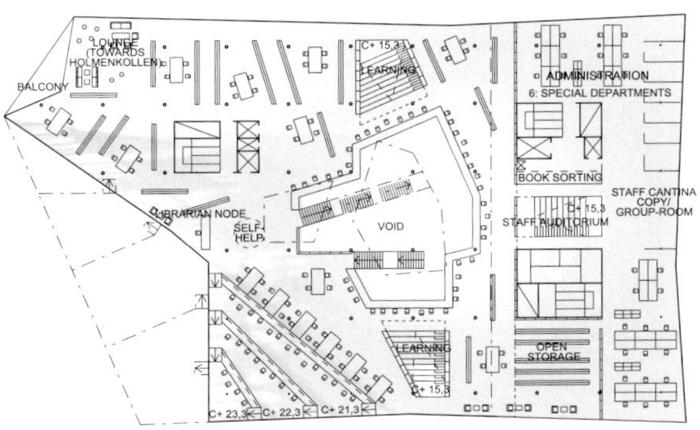

3. Main media / learning The 3rd floor is part of the main media collection and has a lot of good places for working. There are two special learning rooms (auditoriums) above the light shafts and there are other possible separate study rooms. An "oasis" with a view toward Holmenkollen gives a special attraction to the floor.

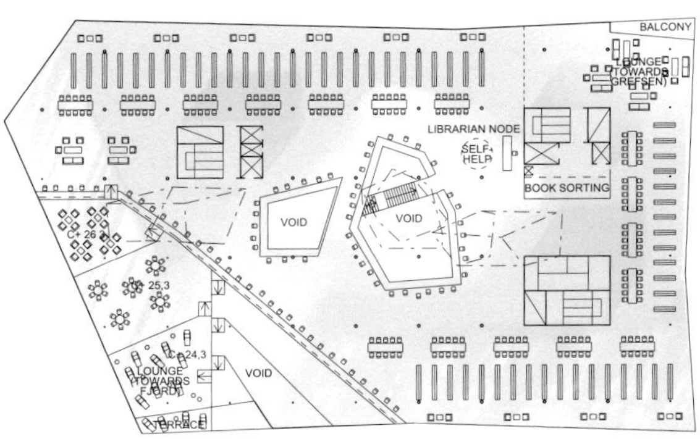

4. Main media / contemplation The top floor (4th floor) has the potential to be the quietest zone in the house. From here you have a beautiful view to the fjord. A terraced part of the floor gives several places for enjoying this view. The terraced floor is the only part in the building which is not totally accessible to handicapped people. A ramp could possibly be implemented. Here is also an "oasis" with a view toward Grefsenkollen. At the same time skylights give a calm atmosphere for studying and contemplation.

The Shining Lamp

Good quality of daylight is essential for a library. We wanted a building that was filled with a soft and comfortable daylight. Deichman Bjørvika's relatively compact volume forms a enough starting point for creating an energy-efficient building, but at the same time it is a challenge to get enough daylight in such a deep structure. The variety and spread of activities in the large, continuous library space required an even distribution of light throughout the interior. The light shafts ensured good light conditions in the mid-area of the upper floors, so the challenge was greatest on the lower floors. At the time we knew of a relatively new product that was both insulating and translucent, so-called nanogel insulation. This provided an opportunity to combine high environmental ambitions with good daylight access. We proposed a facade consisting of a variety of translucent (nanogel) fields and transparent fields of pure glass.

The transparent areas were located where they would provide views on different areas of the city. These viewpoints created different oases in the library, satisfying the need for differentiated places and qualities. The fact that each floor had its own view could serve as an inspiration to explore the building further. The translucent facade filtered the light and filled the interior with a calm and even daylight, creating a contemplative and focused atmosphere that felt sheltered from the busy city outside. It also gave more

The library as a glowing lamp in the city. Illustration from the competition.

focus to the light shafts, which are the heart of the library – the social space that connects people and the library to the city. And as the evening falls, light radiates through the facade, transforming the library into a shining lamp that invites the city's inhabitants into the light and warmth.

Sketch model from the competition.

The competition model being finalized.

EY
AVINOR
HCL
OSLO ATRIUM
nordicCrane

3 Concept Meets Reality

In April 2009, the architectural competition was finally decided and our proposal Diagonale was unanimously named the winner. We did not know then that it would take eleven years before our ideas from the competition were turned into a real building for the people of Oslo. Toward the end of the year, the project gradually came into motion. The company ÅF Advansia was engaged as project managers by the municipality and started the work of engaging the rest of the consultant group. In the meantime we got the opportunity to develop the structure in collaboration with Bollinger+Grohmann and our engineer from the competition, Florian Kosche. With the challenges related to the diagonal light shafts and a cantilever of 20 meters, it was clear that the structure would require special attention from the very beginning.

Simultaneously, the librarians initiated the work of further developing the program based on our winning proposal from the competition. The current library manager Knut Skansen was hired as user coordinator and managed the collaboration between architects and librarians with a steady hand.

In the spring of 2010, the remaining consultants were contracted with Multiconsult at the head of a large association with Bollinger+Grohmann, Hjellnes Consult, Brekke and Strand under the name KulturPlan Bjørvika. Environment and ICT were advertised as separate contracts, and it was Asplan Viak / Kan Energi and Rambøll who received them, respectively. Many specialists had to be in place to develop this project, which is unique in a Norwegian context. Later, Scenario interior architects were also hired, and the design team was complete.

< Images from the construction site.
The construction process lasted from 2014 to 2020.

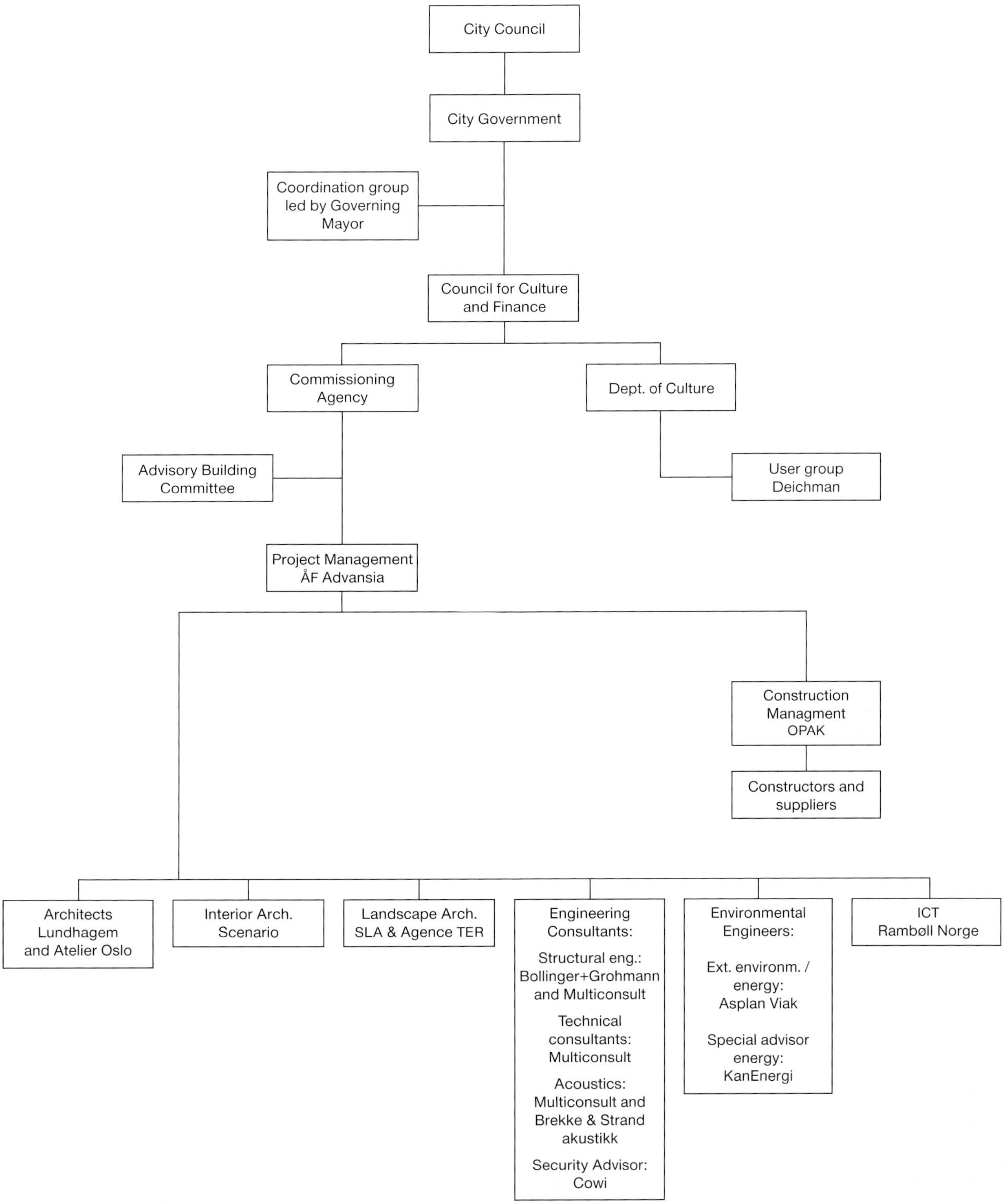

Matrix showing the project as it was organized with all municipal bodies and commisioned companies involved.

The Lasting Framework

As the concept of light shafts developed, the ceilings were already being studied as an element that ought to be of particular importance to the building's architecture. As you move up through the house, your gaze is drawn upward through the light shafts, and the ceilings emerge as an important element. Therefore, we needed to create an interesting ceiling, for instance by making the roof structure and the ceiling one and the same element. Although none of these ideas were fully developed during the competition period, they initiated a process that was taken up again in the further development of the project and which later came to be important for the design of the building's structure and ceilings.

A competition proposal that was based on cantilevers, and at the same time had areas with diagonal light shafts where columns were unwanted, was a demanding and exciting starting point for our development of a structural concept.

During the winter of 2009/10, we had several working meetings with the engineers from Bollinger Grohmann about different ways to solve the structure. Our ambition was to develop a concept that not only would solve our structural challenges but could also become an important architectural element, a structure that gave the building identity and atmosphere. Since the library would be an institution in continuous change, it was important for us that the structure would be a lasting element and quality throughout the life of the building.

We started by exploring several different relevant principles that could respond to the structural challenges.

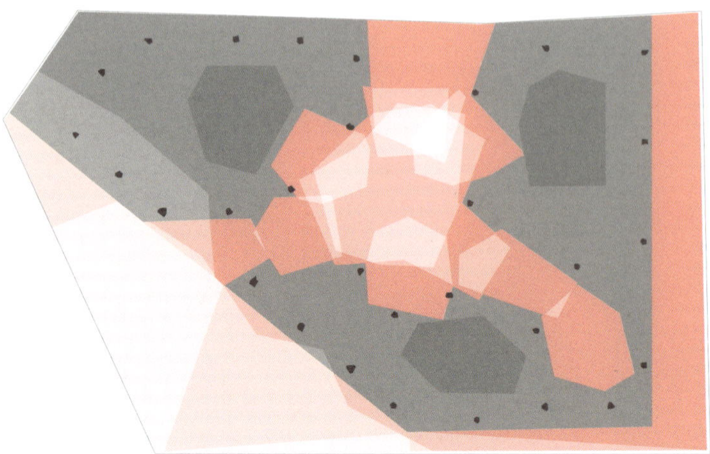

Diagram that highlights the constructive challenges of the building. The cantilevered areas in the periphery and the light shaft areas in the middle where columns were not desirable, marked in red.

> Picture from the two architectural offices' inspection when the concrete core structure was finally completed in 2017.

Early sketches from Bollinger+Grohmann of a system that worked from the inside like a tree with cantilevered branches.

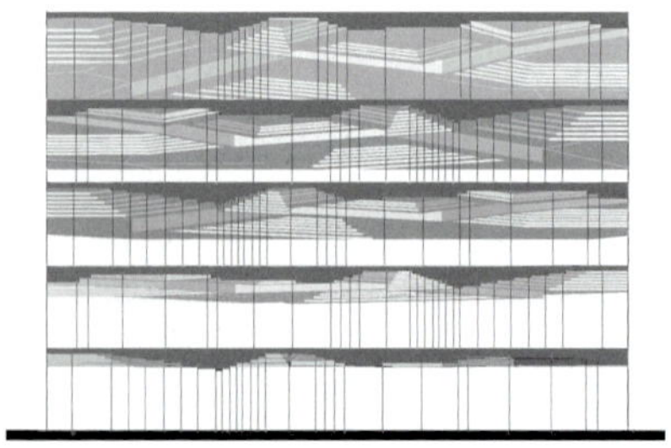

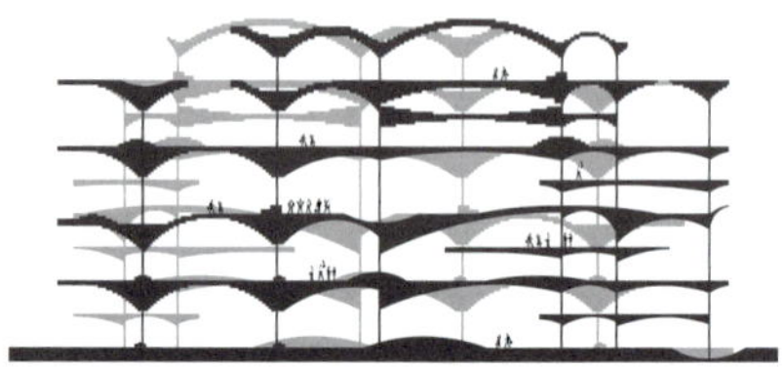

Sketches from the competition showing structures built with layers of structural ceilings. These ideas were brought up again in the further development of the project.

Studies of cantilevered systems with beam and column structures.

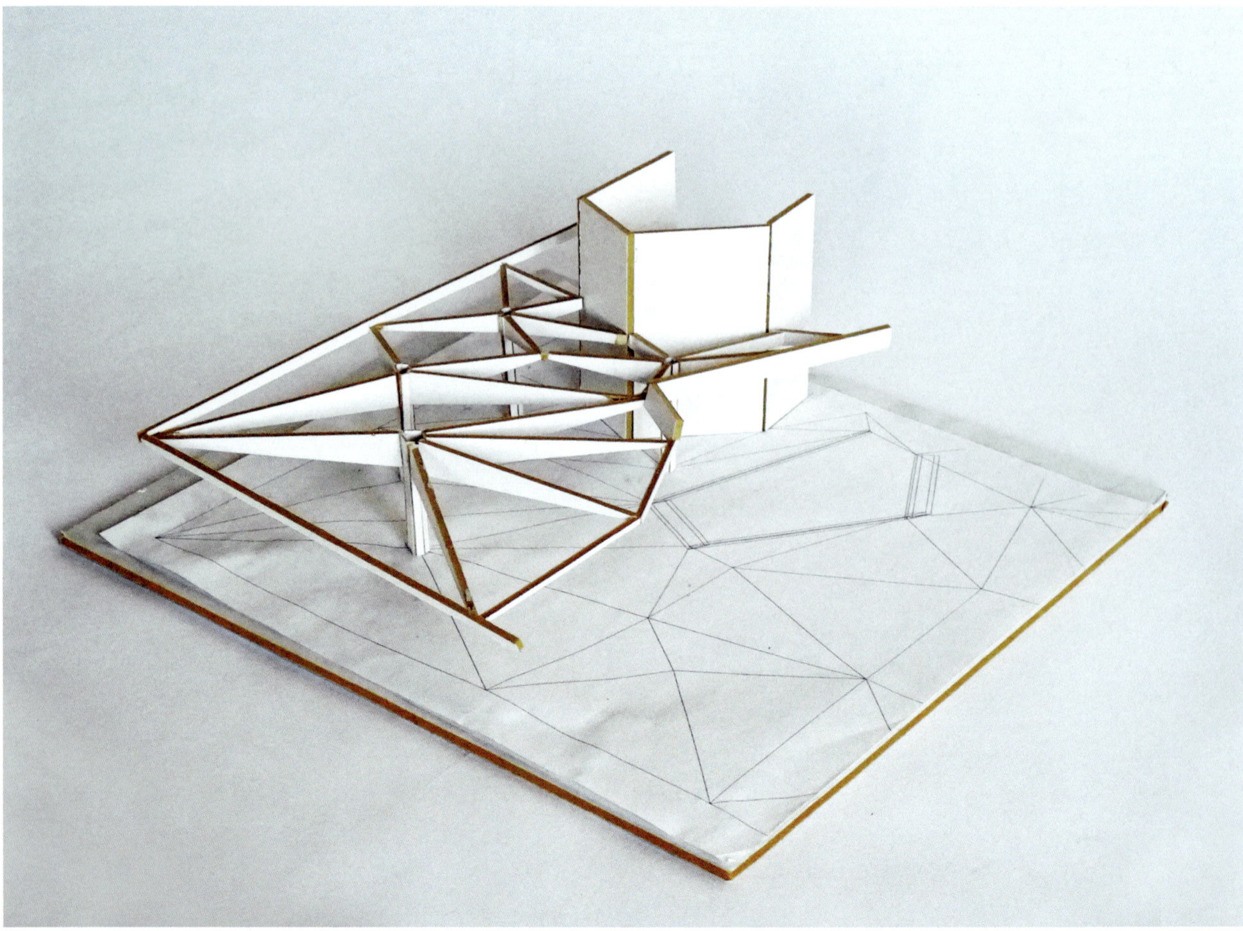

Sketch models of slabs where the structural height is optimized in different ways that form spatial structures.

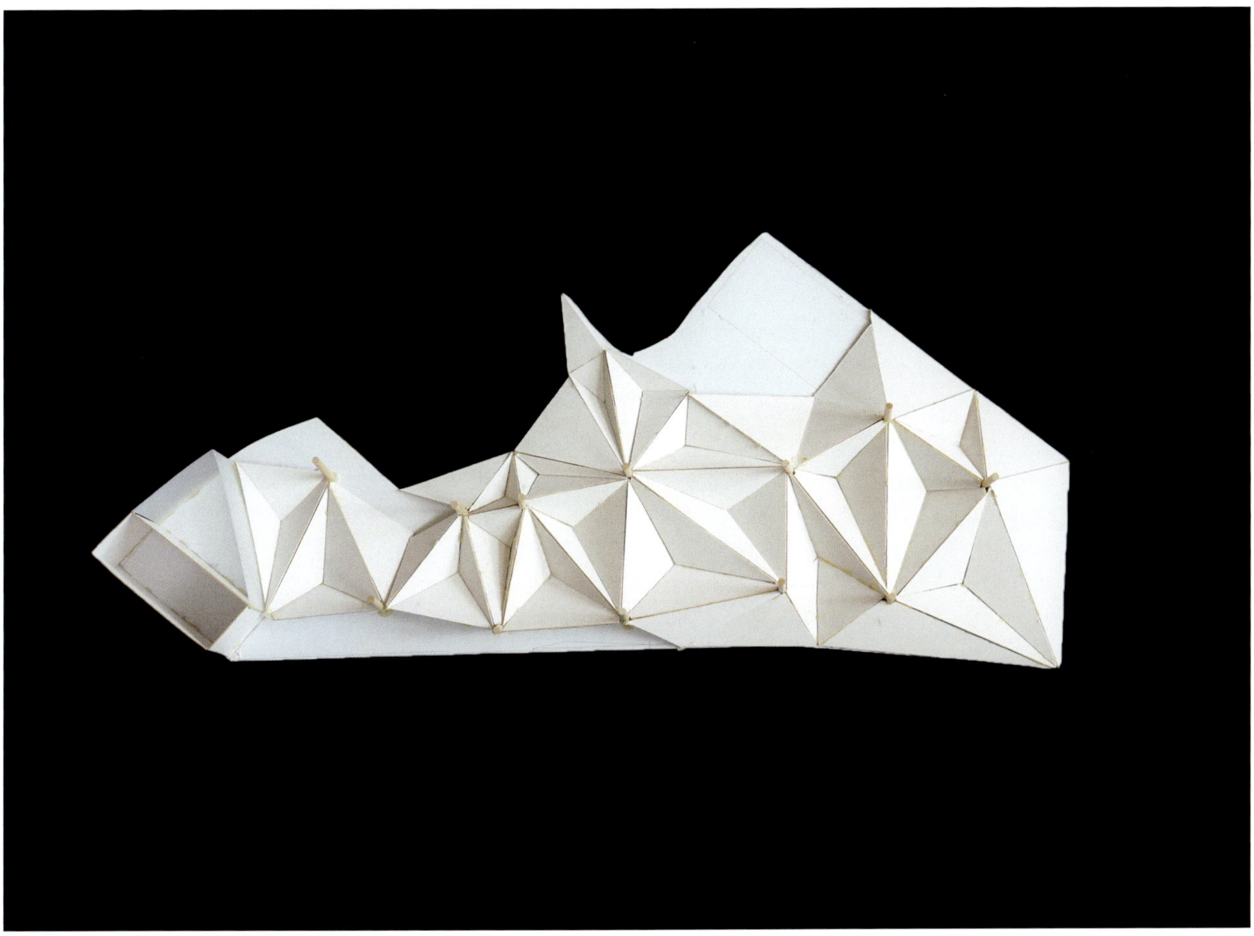

After a lengthy process in which many proposals were tested and rejected, we summarized the initial studies in two main alternative principles:

1 A truss system, where the structure is located in the periphery of the building (integrated in the facade).
2 A system based on cantilevering, with cantilevered, folded concrete slabs.

After evaluating these two structural principles, we decided to move on with the system of a folded concrete slab. The idea of a cantilevered structural system supported the building's idea and solved the interior and the different floors meeting with the light shafts in a good way. The system was based on a series of cantilevered "concrete mushrooms." The principle works by folding the concrete slab to a geometry that gives the slab the necessary strength to handle large and small cantilevers. The height of the fold is determined by the strength required. Together with the engineers, we were thus able to form a roof with optimized geometry in relation to structural strength. This method gives the slab a stiffness up to 10 times stronger than a normal flat concrete slab. The building's folded concrete slab structure is now regarded as a unique engineering achievement.

Study of how the folded slabs meet the light shafts. Illustration where you look upward toward the sky through the layers with structural ceilings. We sought to maintain this effect even after going over to the folded slab only in the roof, by having special concrete parapets as endings toward the light shafts.

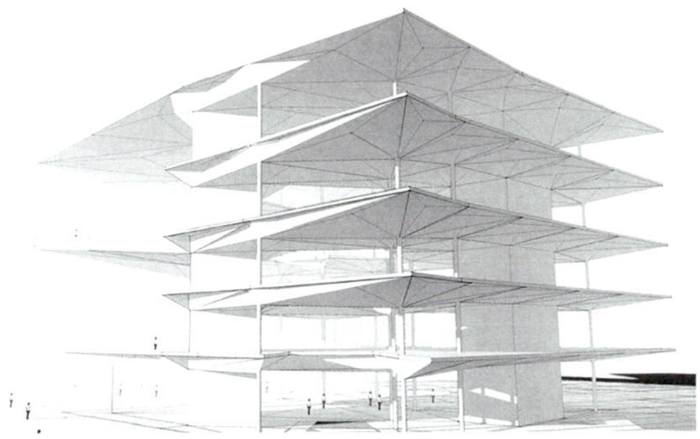

The search for a global structural system. The first studies led to two main alternatives, one system based on trusses in the facade (top) and one based on cantilevered decks (bottom).

The ceiling like a forest. Different layers of foliage open up to the sky. An image that inspired us to work with different layers of ceilings upward to strengthen the experience of the light shafts.

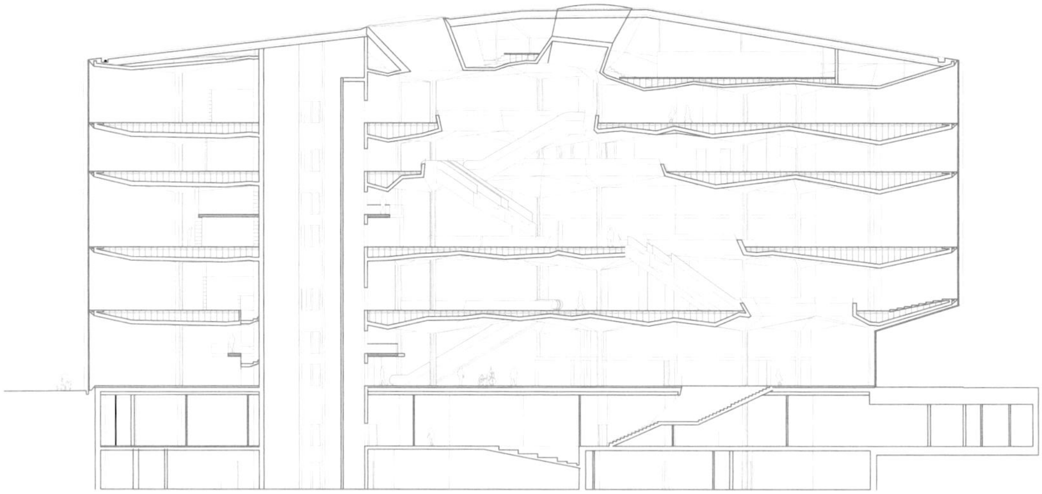

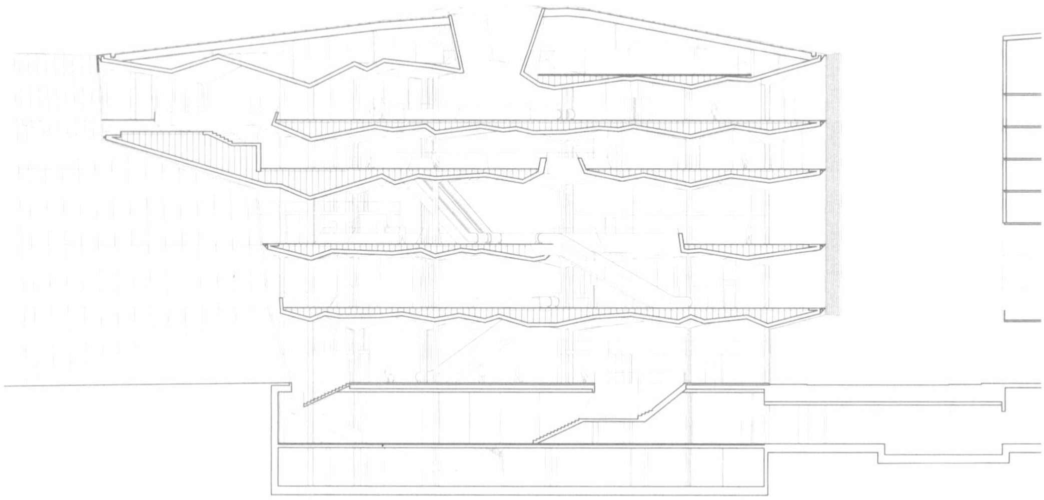

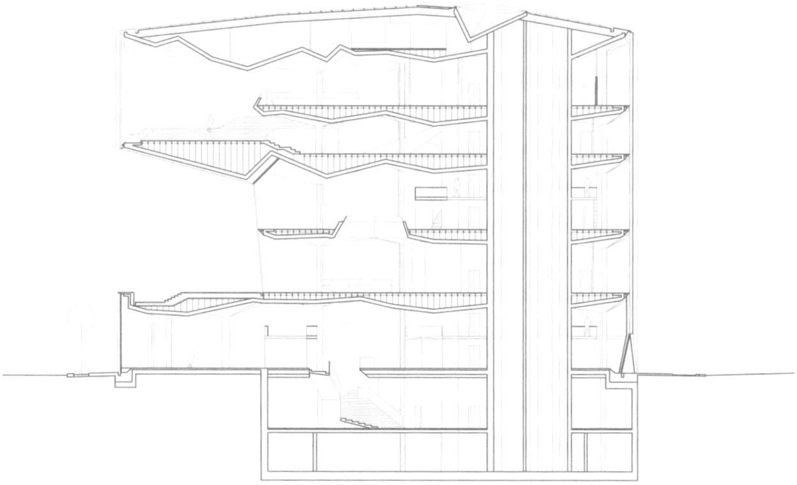

Section and model pictures of the first draft, where all the slabs were based on the folded slab principle. This was later simplified due to cost savings.

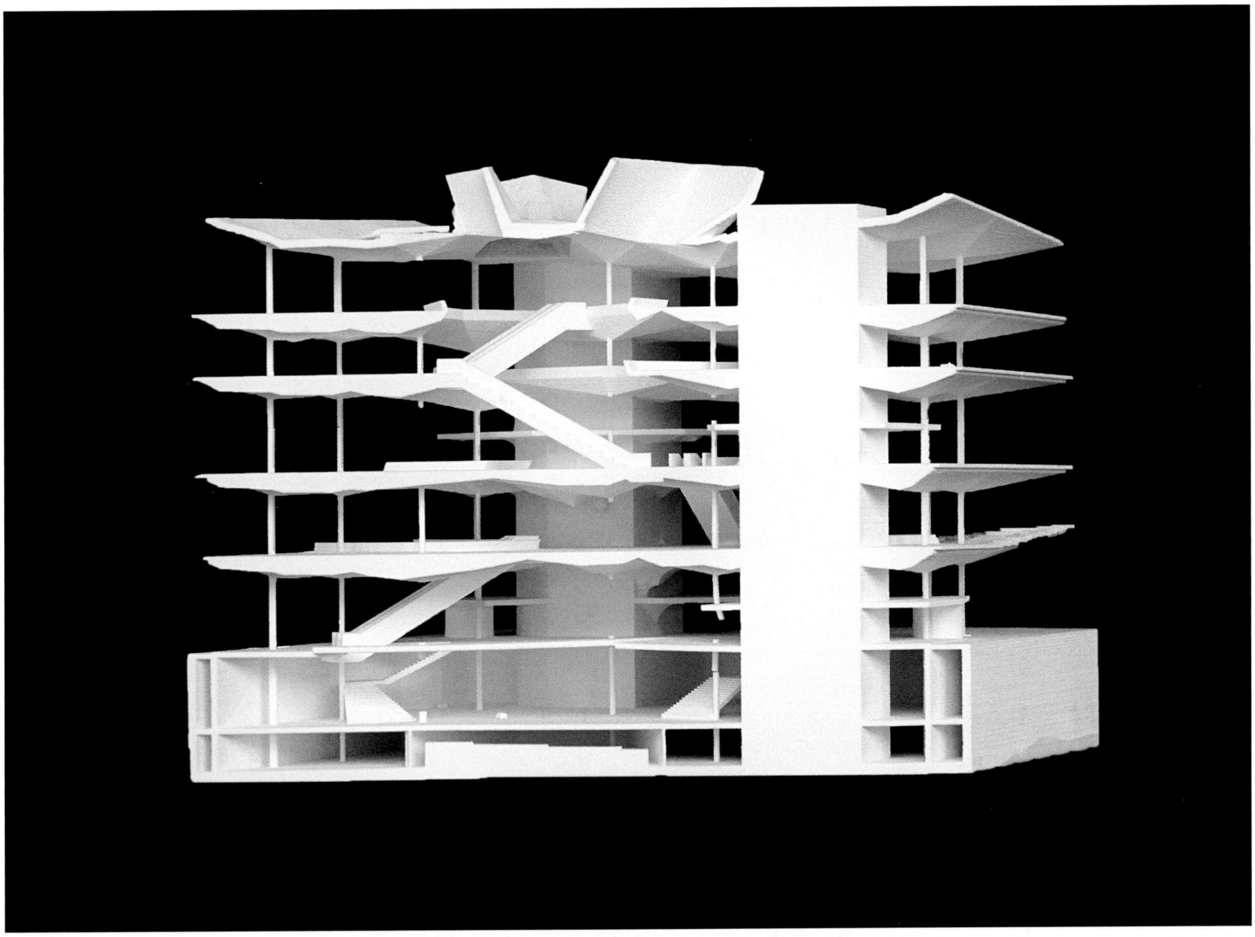

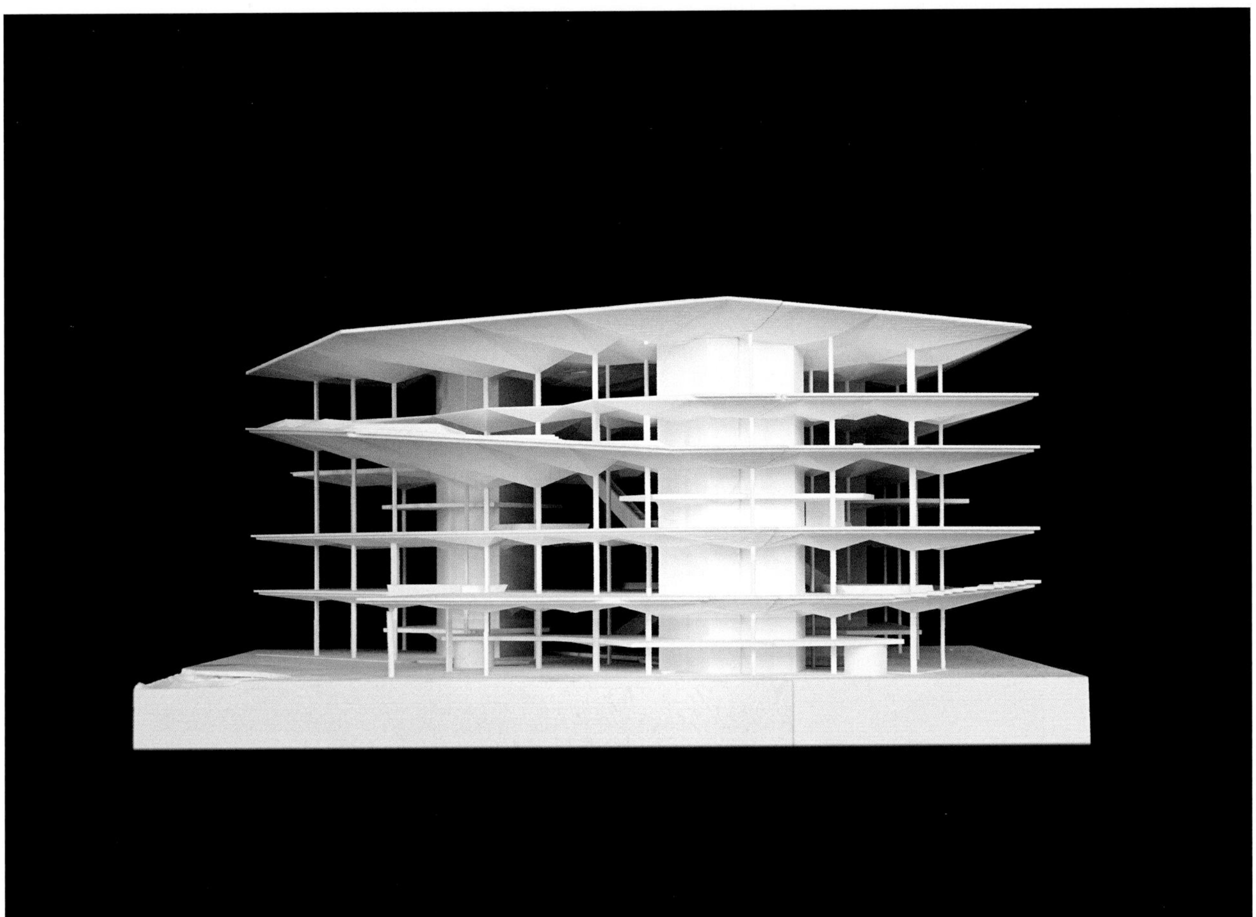

In the first draft, each slab worked individually and created a three-dimensional roof landscape on all floors. This turned out to be too expensive, so the system had to be simplified. Eventually, only the upper slab, the building's actual roof structure, was designed with a folded concrete slab, while the cantilevers on the other floors were hung up in thin steel rods from this. The columns were placed in a zone around the cores and at a good distance from the facade. It was important to us that the pillars did not stand in a straight row but were given a natural position in relation to the surrounding spaces. The cross section (diameter) was optimized for the load that the individual columns had to handle. The fact that the columns have a varying cross section and are not in line creates a more organic and informal atmosphere for the library space. The further process of realizing the folded slab structure required great commitment from engineers, project management, construction management, and contractor. An enormous puzzle of a formwork was prefabricated in Austria. This ensured millimeter precision on the construction site and made it possible to build the demanding mold in a relatively rational way. The contractor also made several 1:1 mock-ups where, among other things, the concrete recipes were tested to make sure that the concrete would not be too liquid when it was poured into the inclined molds.

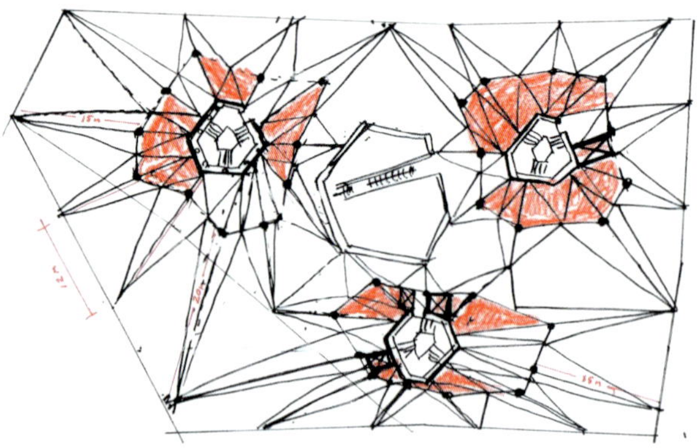

Early sketch of the folded slab with the small, specialized rooms organized around the cores.

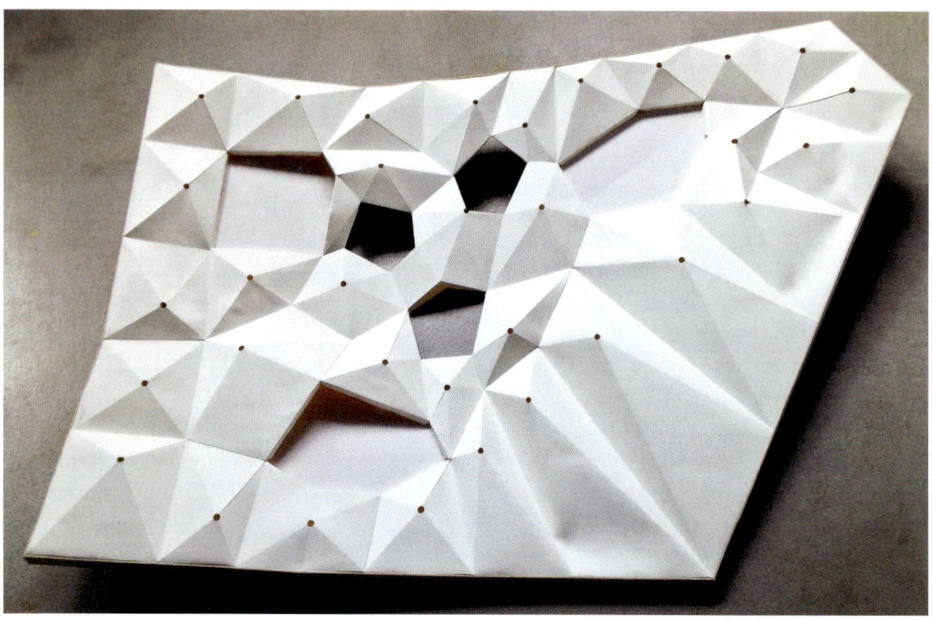

Model studies of the folded slab.

> Illustration of the central space where the light shafts meet (with folded slab on all floors).

Overview of the structural elements of the folded slab and how other slabs are hung up to handle the cantilevers. (Illustration: Bollinger+Grohmann)

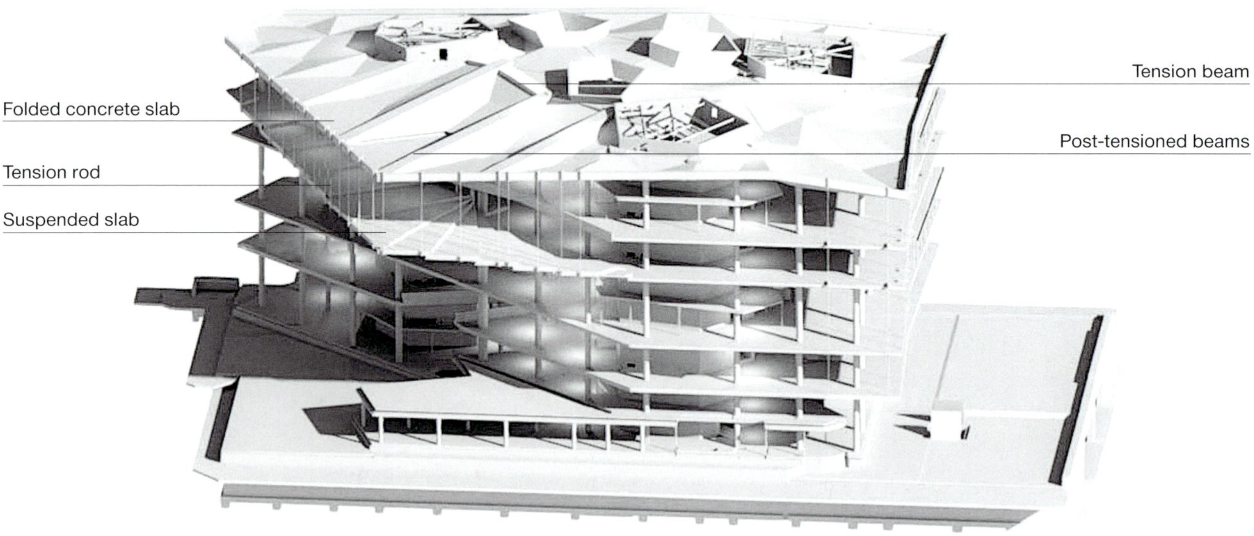

Diagrams below from Bollinger+Grohmann showing the structural principles of the folded slab.

1. The global structural system and the connection between the folded concrete slab and the suspended slabs.
2. The static principle of the folded slab. The global bending moment is divided in tension- and compression forces.
3. Compression forces in the folded slab.
4. Tension forces in the folded slab.

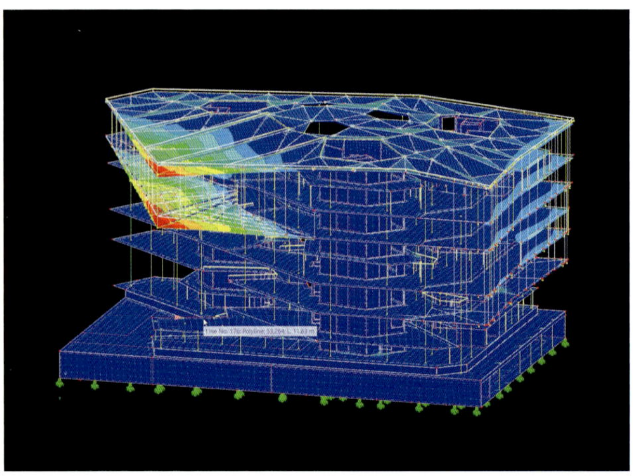

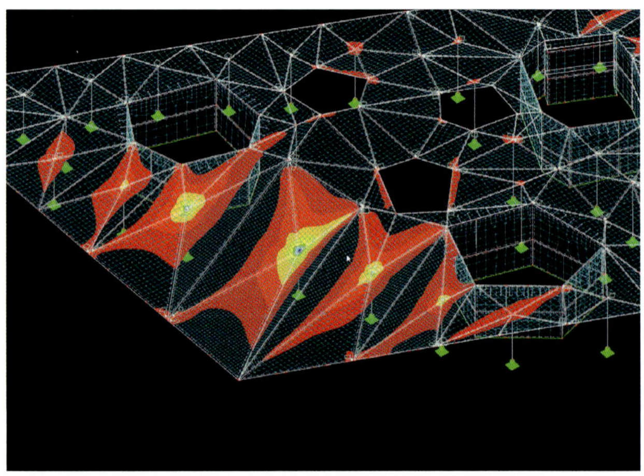

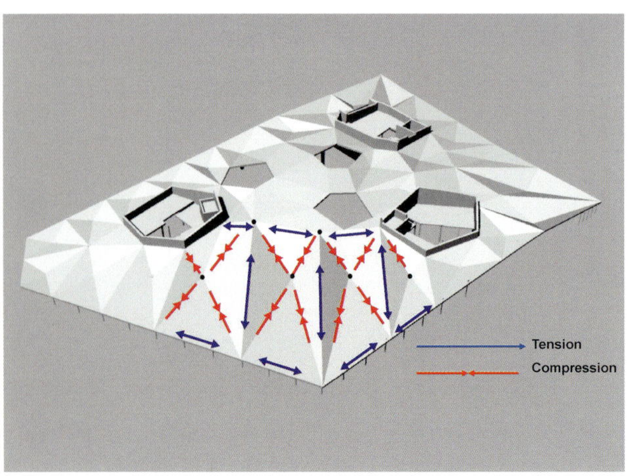

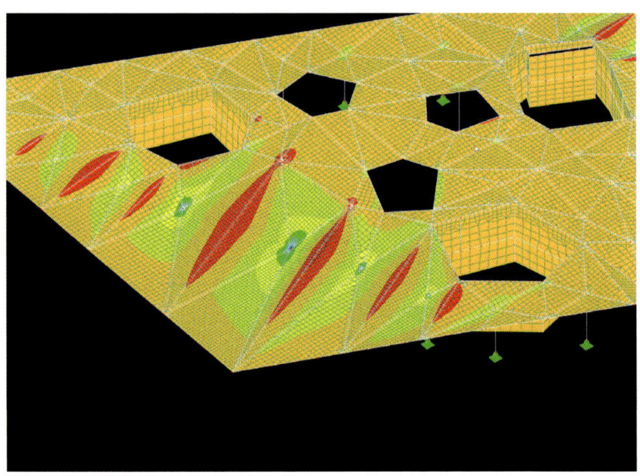

Prefabricated elements from Austria
arrive at the construction site.

The big puzzle is finally ready for
reinforcement and casting.

In the other slabs, a system called BubbleDeck was introduced, where air bubbles inside the concrete creates a biaxial hollow slab with a great structural strength, at the same time as far less concrete is used. The slab cooperates with the concrete parapets around the light shafts to provide large spans and the freedom to avoid columns in the areas affected by the diagonal light shafts. The structural concrete parapets create a spatial connection in the light shafts and direct the gaze up toward the folded concrete slab with the skylights. Both the folded slab and the BubbleDeck are examples of structures that use geometry to achieve strength and thus significantly reduce the use of materials. Together with the use of a newly developed low-carbon concrete with recycled aggregate, as well as recycled steel in the reinforcement, this was an important contribution to reducing the total greenhouse gas emissions for the building by almost 70 percent compared to similar reference projects.

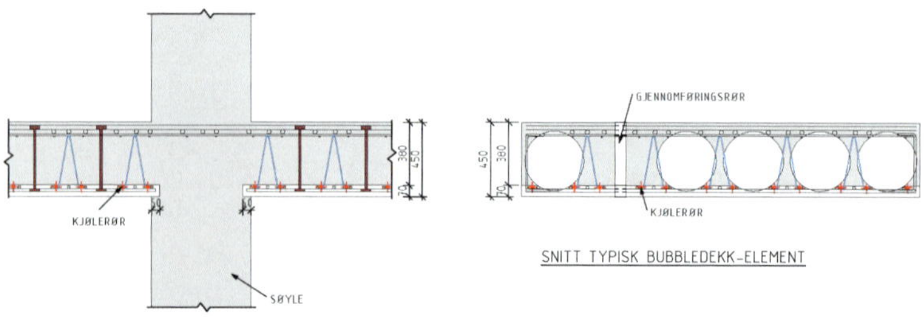

Typical section through the other slabs that were changed to a construction of BubbleDeck. This provided an effective slab that could handle the large spans that the limitations in column placement provided. (Illustration: Multiconsult)

Image of work on the construction site where the bubbles in the BubbleDeck can be seen before casting.

The concrete parapets around the light shafts in the BubbleDecks were important for maintaining a visual connection in the light shafts and connection to the folded slab. They also played an important role as a structural edging beam for the BubbleDeck around the light shafts. (Illustration: Multiconsult)

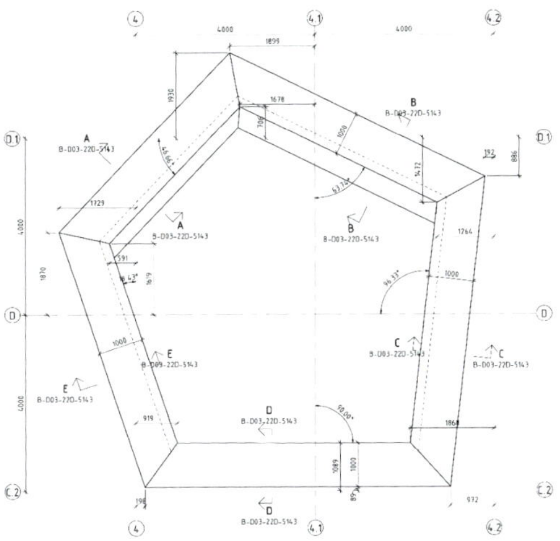

BRYSTNING 1 DEKKE OVER PLAN 2
1:50

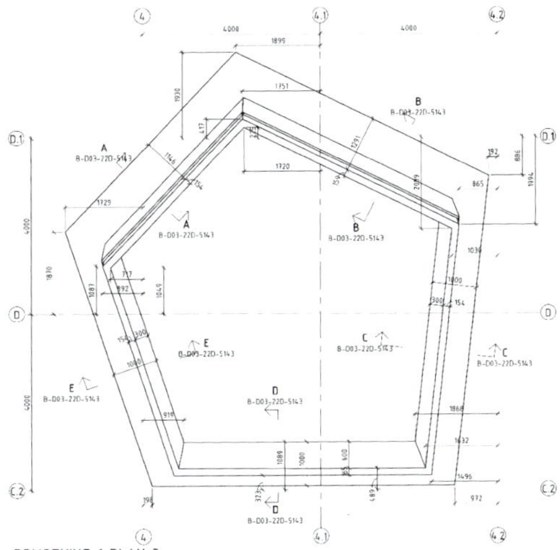

BRYSTNING 1 PLAN 3
1:50

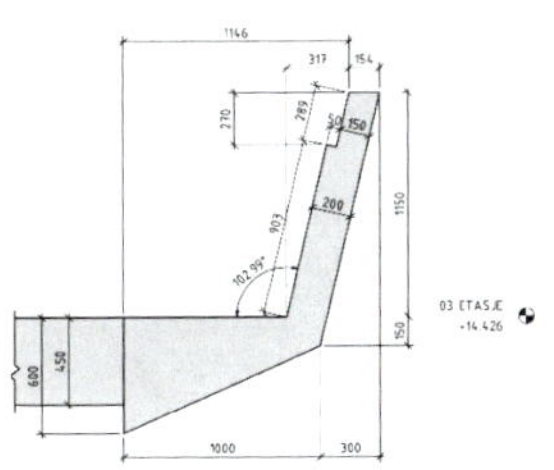

BRYSTNING 1 PLAN 3 – SNITT A

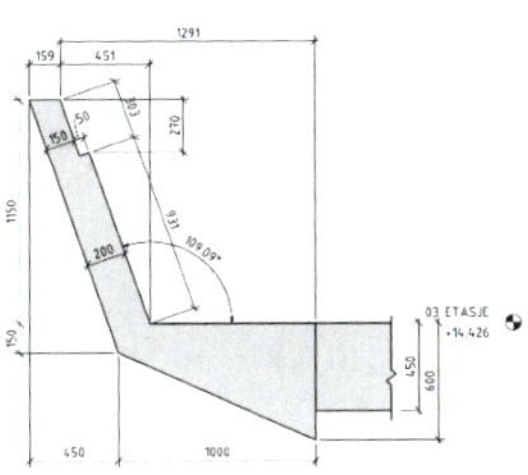

BRYSTNING 1 PLAN 3 – SNITT B

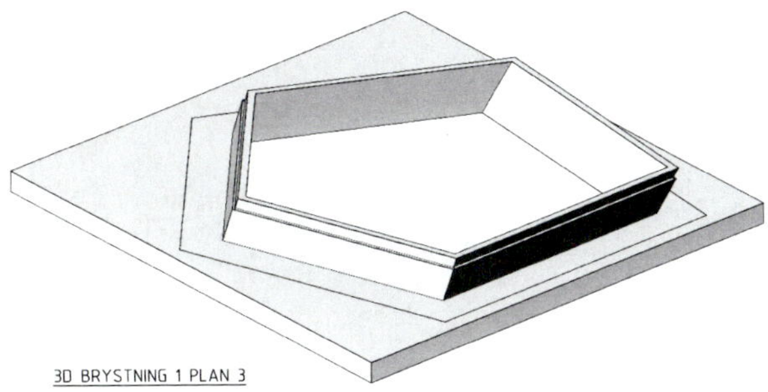

3D BRYSTNING 1 PLAN 3

1:1 mock-up of concrete parapet.

Ground conditions in Bjørvika are demanding and the site for the Deichman Bjørvika was no exception. It consisted of old embankments and deposits above a dense layer of clay that was located 15–20 meters below ground level and had a water intrusion into the construction site of up to 400 liters per second. The old embankments had an open structure, which meant that the water level in the pit corresponded to sea level and driving sheet piles through it was especially demanding.

The project thus faced great challenges with water penetration into the construction pit, a problem it took a long time to get control of. This led to enormous, extraordinary groundwork costs and a long and tenacious process to get above the ground. The building has a watertight basement construction, where it took 13,000 meters of piles to reach 60–70 meters down to bedrock.

It was demanding to secure a watertight building pit. In the end experts from the Netherlands were called upon to provide watertight sheet piles. The challenging ground conditions led to great delays and increased costs for the project.

Drawing from the engineers, which shows the construction's relation to the ground. The ground conditions in Bjørvika were challenging, with piling that had to go through various historical harbor fronts down to a sloping bedrock. (Illustration: Multiconsult)

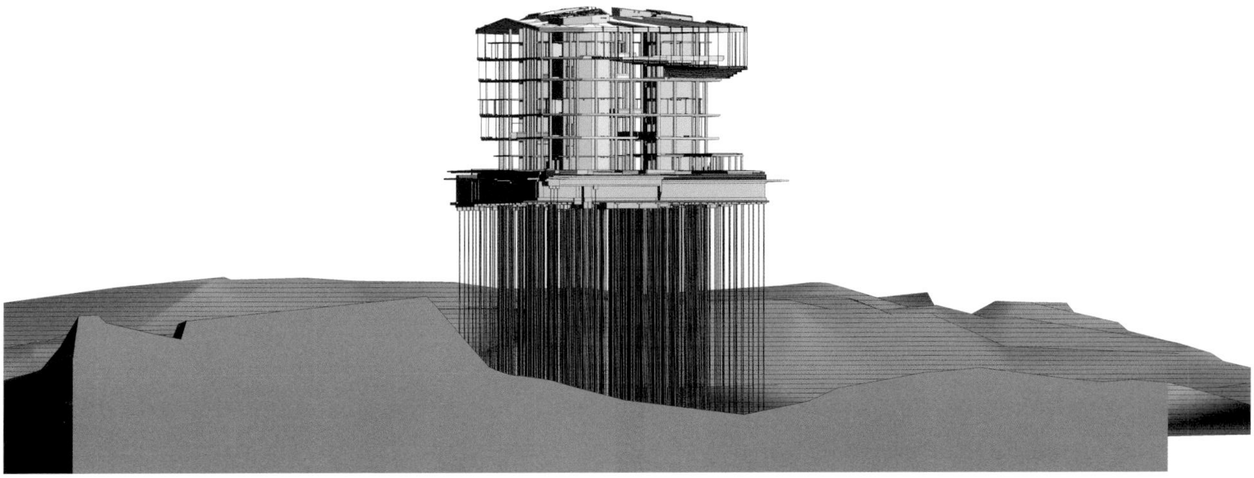

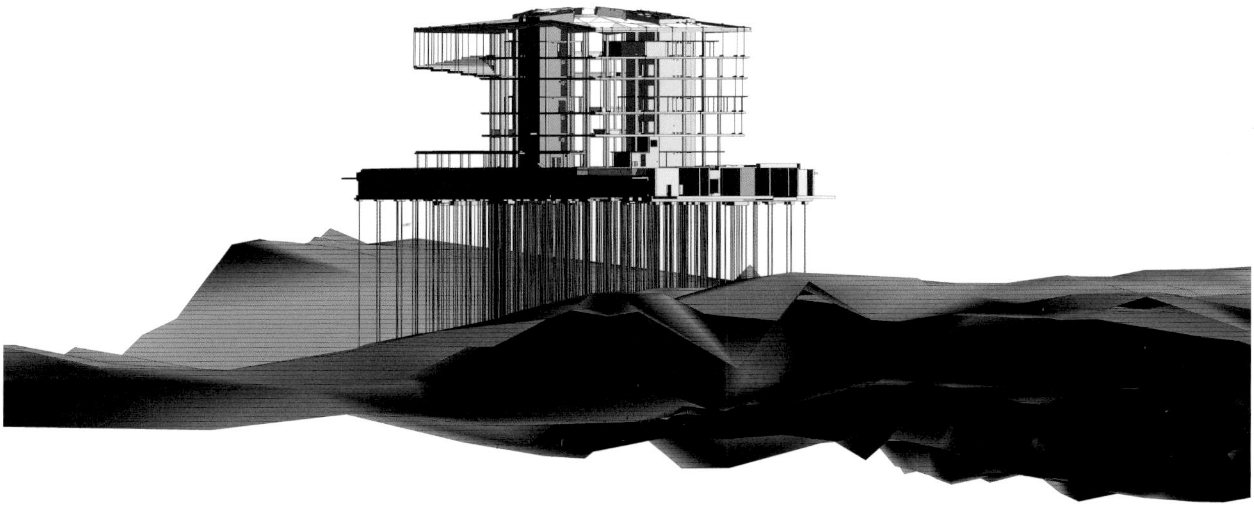

Concrete parapets around light shafts
Detailed section 1:25

1 Glass railings
2 Worktable, hot-rolled steel with linoleum
3 Concrete parapet
4 Floor element, demountable
5 Structure for raised floor
6 Sprinkler pipes
7 Electrical ducts
8 Sprinkler head
9 BubbleDeck (biaxial concrete slab)
10 Acoustic baffle ceiling
11 Raised floor / air chamber for ventilation

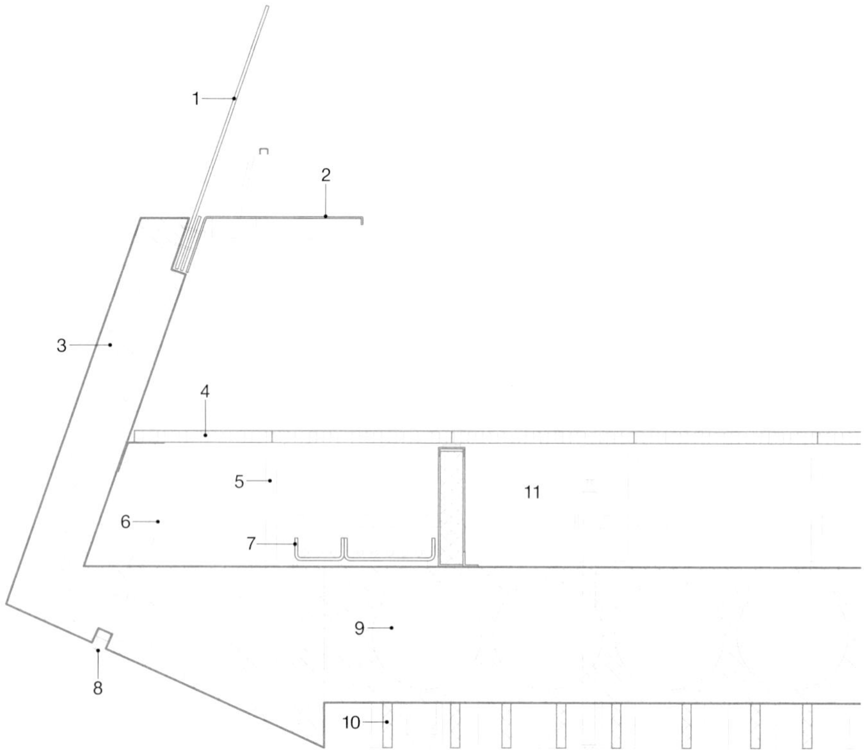

Sections that show variation of angles to adapt to the direction of the light shafts.

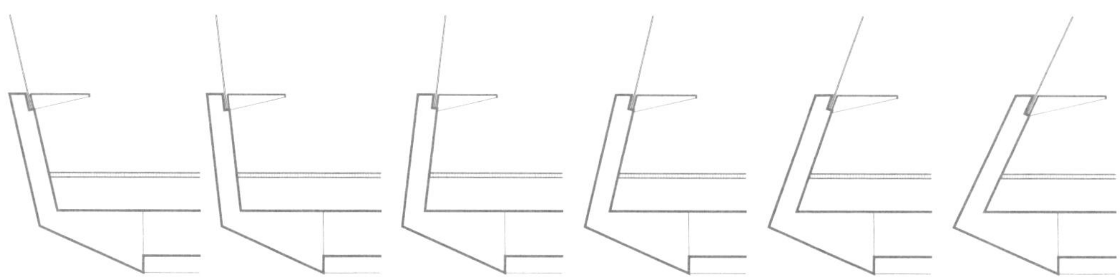

Folded slab
Axonometric section 1:150

1 Roof membrane, light gray
2 Insulation, mineral wool
3 Steel structure
4 Space for technical installations
5 Folded concrete slab
6 Concrete columns
7 TRP, corrugated steel plates
8 Recessed acoustic ceiling, "stretch ceiling"

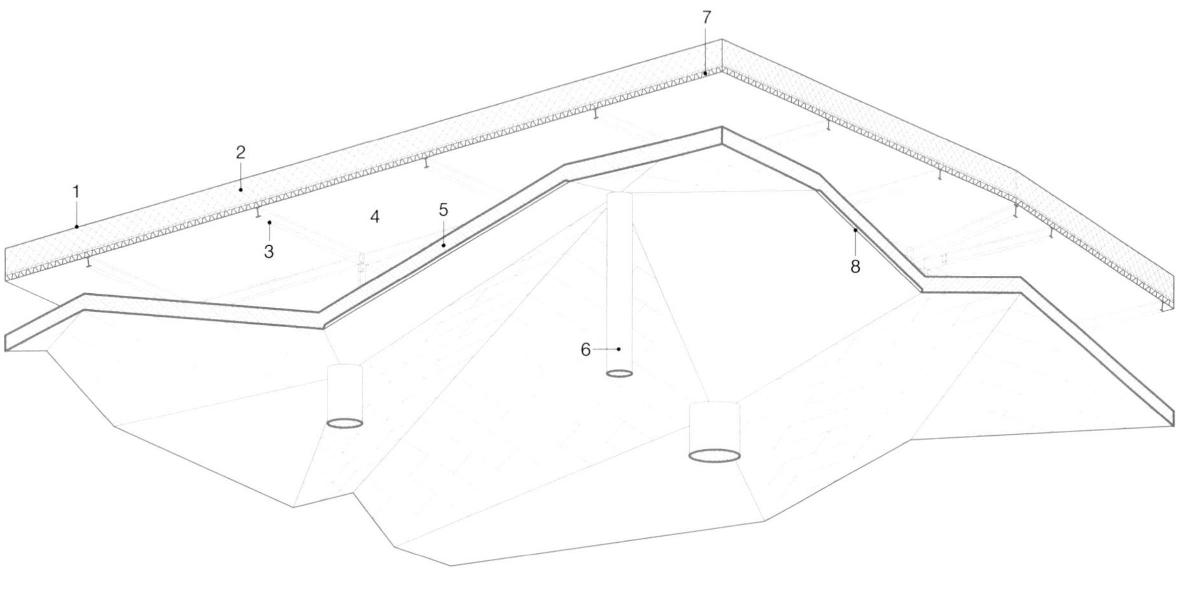

CARL DEICHMAN-SAMLINGEN
Navn og slekt
Names and Genealogy
Navn og slekt

Skylight
Detailed section 1:25

1 Insulated glass panels with integrated aluminum mesh for sun protection
2 Steel structure for glass panels
3 Ventilation hatch
4 Sprinkler
5 Roof membrane, light gray
6 Heating cables in gutter
7 Insulation, pressure-resistant mineral wool
8 TRP, corrugated steel plates
9 Steel structure
10 Folded concrete slab

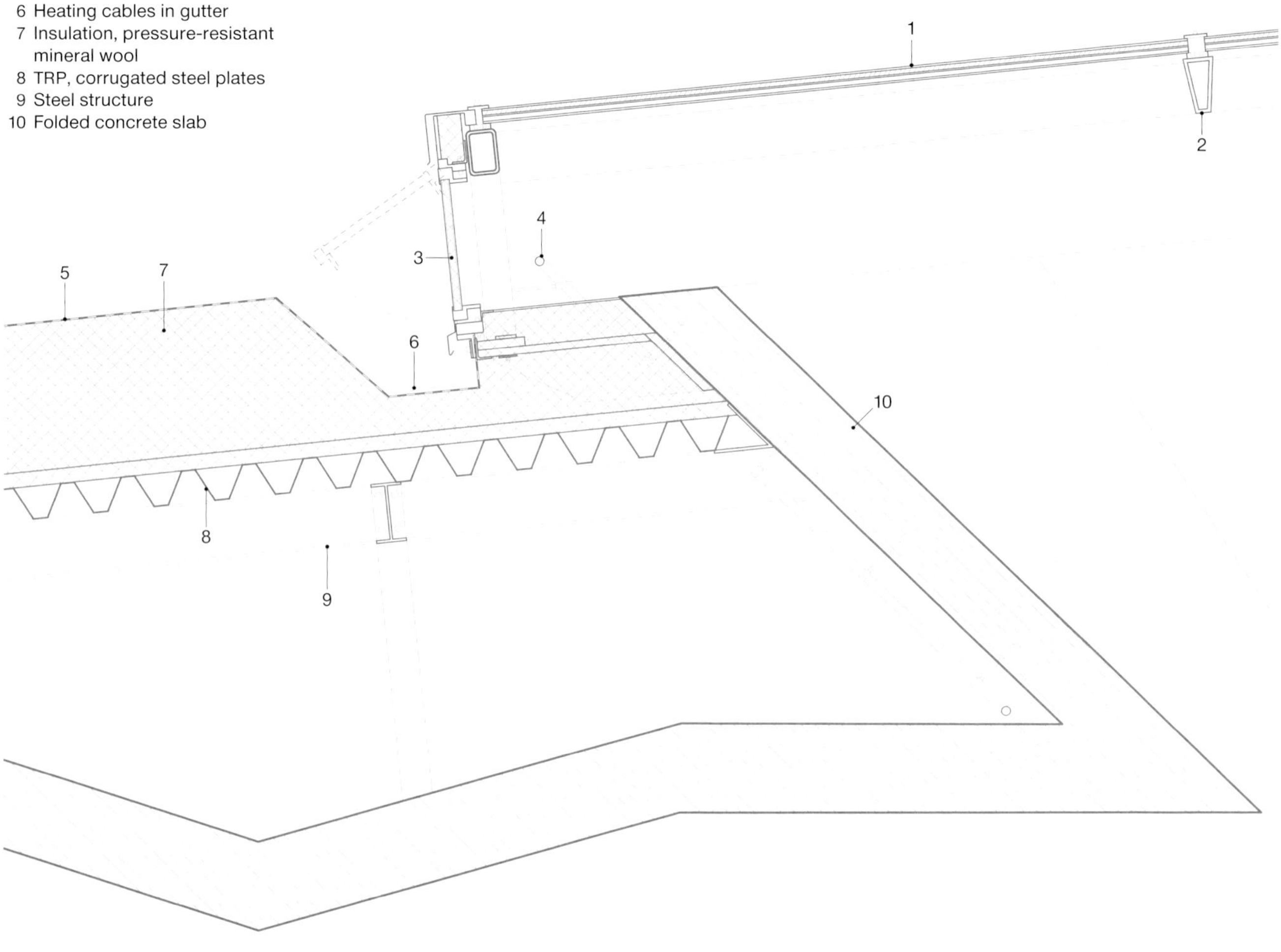

Typical section of skylight.

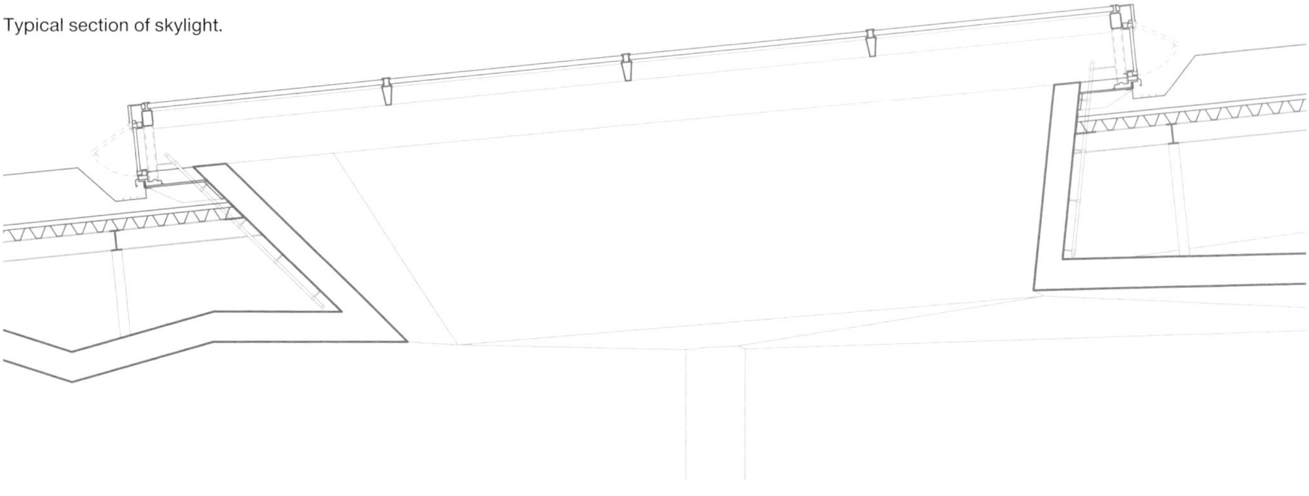

The Ceiling above Us

Already in the competition phase we had imagined that the ceilings would be a main element defining the spatial atmosphere in the library. Considering that a library will change its function and content repeatedly during the building's life cycle, we thought it important to have some fixed elements that in addition to the building's structure would give it a more lasting atmosphere. We had to discard folded slabs on all floors, but the ambition for beautiful ceilings was still there. To achieve this, it was important to get all technical infrastructure down into the floor instead of in the ceiling, which is most common in the Norwegian construction industry. After several years of studies, inspections of reference buildings and discussions within the design group, this was finally decided. By having ventilation and other technical infrastructure in the floor, one could develop a fixed ceiling. At the same time, all the infrastructure became easily accessible in a raised floor, a so-called installation floor, which provides greater flexibility.

Another significant factor was that this principle could help to reduce the building's energy consumption significantly. Instead of traditional ventilation ducts, we could now use the entire cavity in the raised floor as a large air chamber to transport the ventilation air. Forcing the air through narrow ventilation pipes requires significantly more fan energy than a large air chamber, where the air flows with less resistance.

Studies of ceilings in libraries. Historically, ceilings have been important for the identity and atmosphere of many libraries.

With all the technical infrastructure in the floor, there was a potential of exposing the concrete structure in the ceiling, taking advantage of the energy-efficient cooling effect of the thermal mass. This effect is enhanced by cooling pipes cast into the concrete, the so called TABS system, thermo activated slabs. At the same time, the ceiling had to be very absorbent in order to secure the acoustic conditions the library needed to achieve its ambition of arranging parallel activities and being a place where it was not necessary to be quiet.

It was an exciting challenge to develop a ceiling that would expose most of the concrete slab for cooling while also satisfying the building's acoustic needs. We arrived at a ceiling that consisted of a fine-mesh pattern made of an acoustic absorbent, like a baffle ceiling. This baffle ceiling gave us a large enough absorbent surface, leaving a large part of the concrete exposed.

In the folded slab at the top, about half of the triangles formed by the geometry were cast with a recess so that absorbent materials could be fitted here as well. The acoustics in the building have subsequently proved to be excellent and absolutely crucial for the library to function as envisaged, with many parallel activities taking place at the same time.

< Old Deichman library at Hammersborg
Berlin State Library
Bibliotheca Alexandrina
Tama Art University Library
Exeter Library
National Library of France

Seattle Public Library
Koo Chen-Fu Memorial Library
Viipuri Library
New York Public Library
George Peabody Library
Deichman Bjørvika

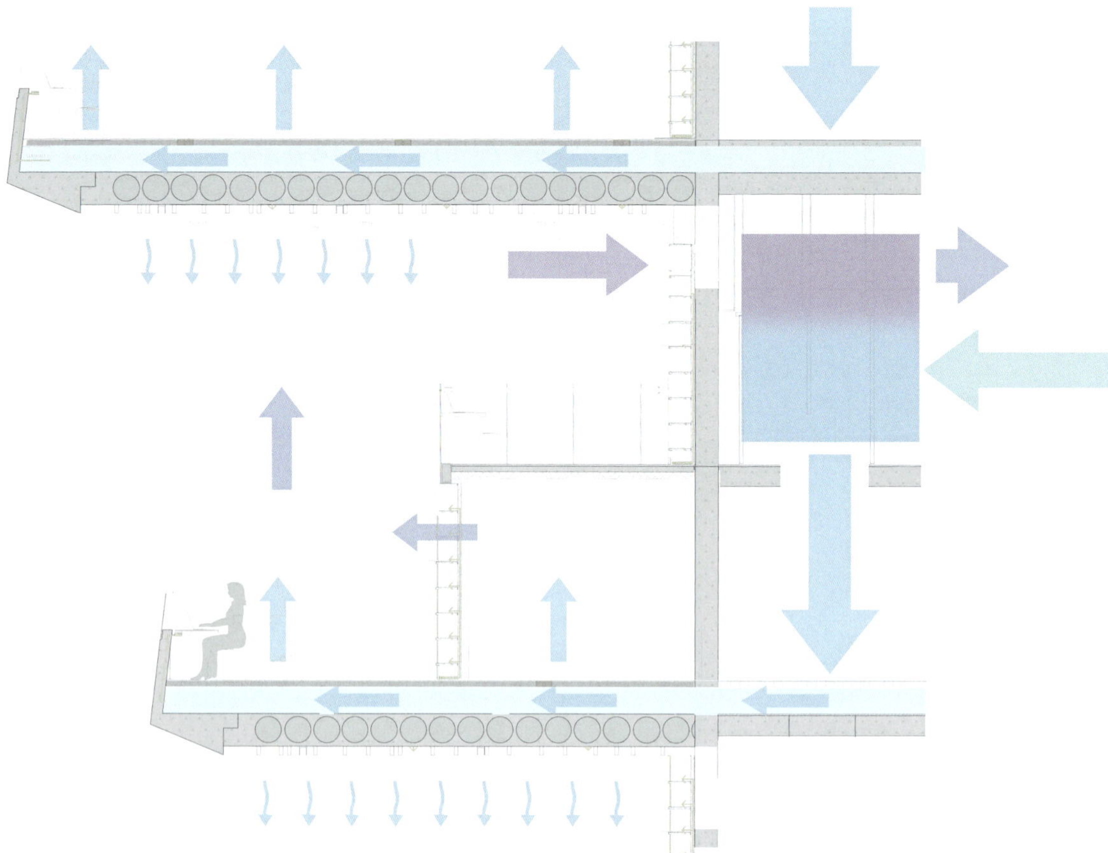

Principle for ventilation and cooling of the building. The raised floor is used as a pressure chamber distributing fresh air. By placing cooling pipes in the concrete, the cooling effect of the thermal mass of the concrete is enhanced.

First attempt at development of a prototype for the baffle ceiling. Here, the baffles were produced from watercut mineral wool. The absorption from these was measured and the results used in the first evaluations done by the acoustic engineers.

Trip to Lindner, who produced the final solution for the baffle ceiling. In the middle a piece of the concrete structure that we brought to ensure that the color tone of the baffle ceiling matched the main structure.

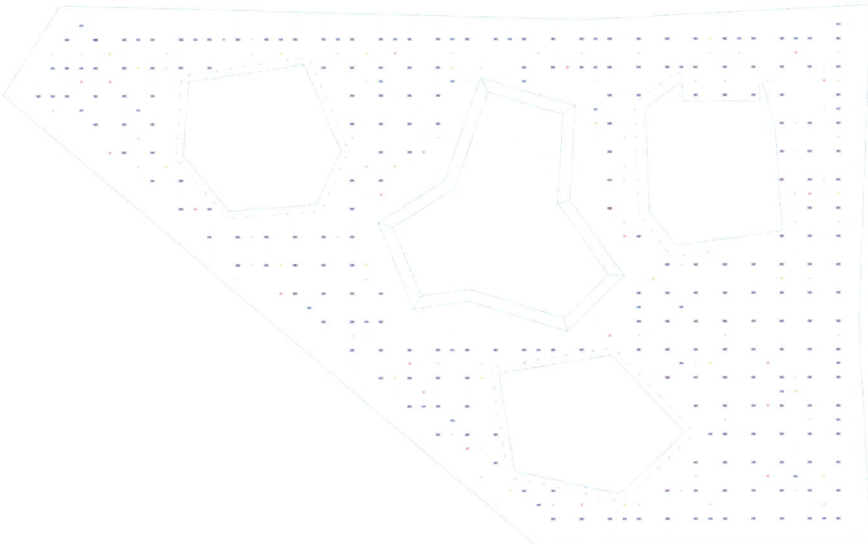

Diagram that shows all the technical elements that had to be integrated into the fixed baffle ceiling.

From the mounting of the installation floor. The floor is raised approximately 450 mm to make sufficient space for technical infrastructure, and at the same time function as a huge air chamber for the ventilation air.

Studies of different geometries on the baffle ceiling. The geometry had to handle the angled geometry of the building and at the same time integrate lighting fixtures and other technical equipment in a natural way.

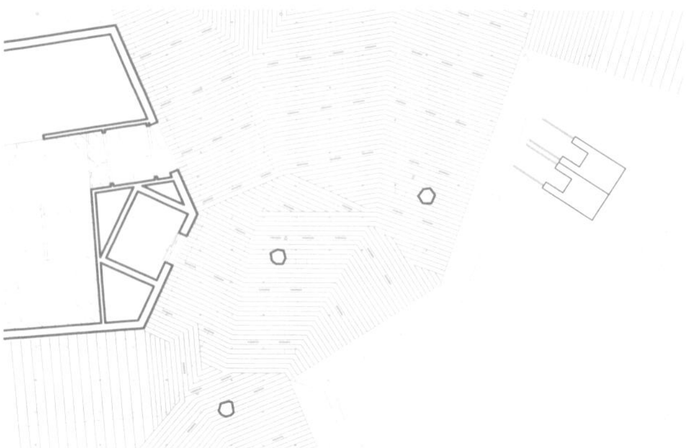

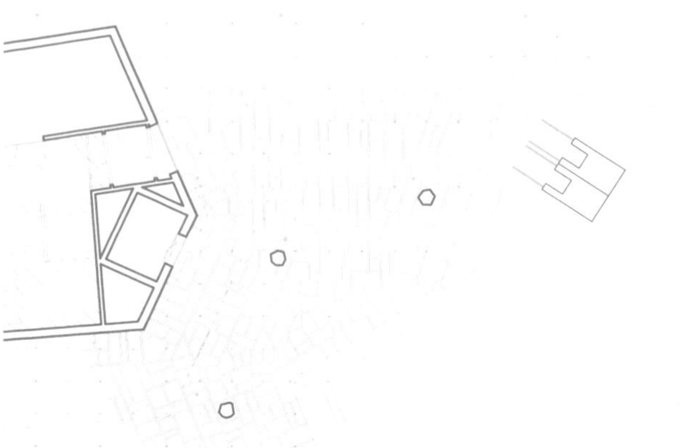

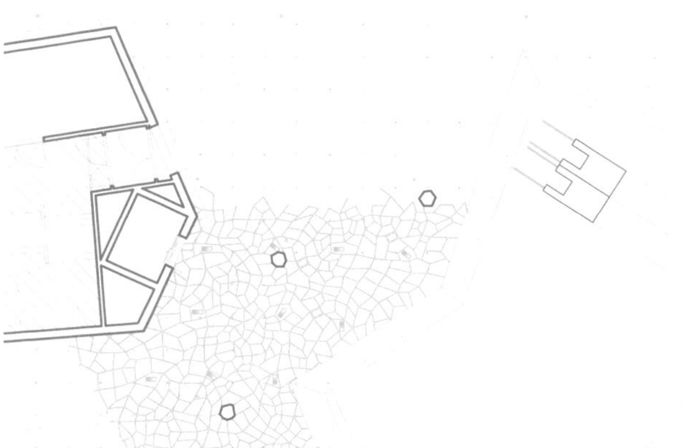

Axonometric of the two different ceiling elements.

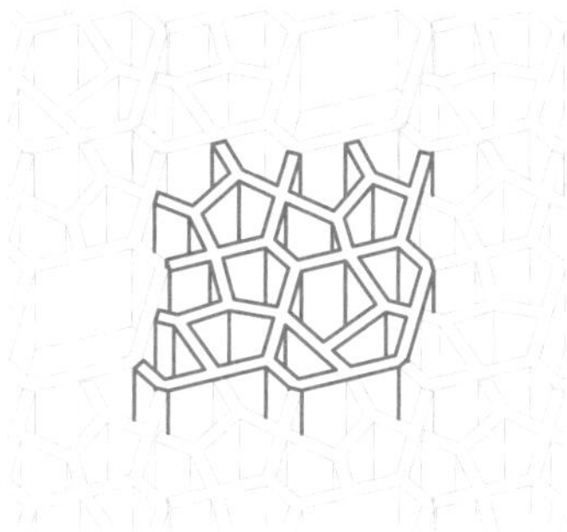

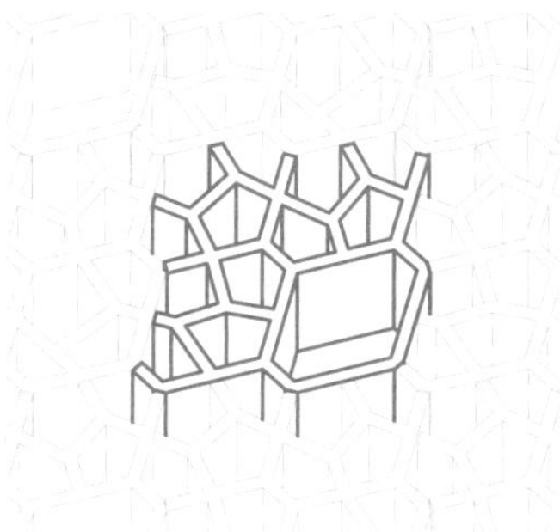

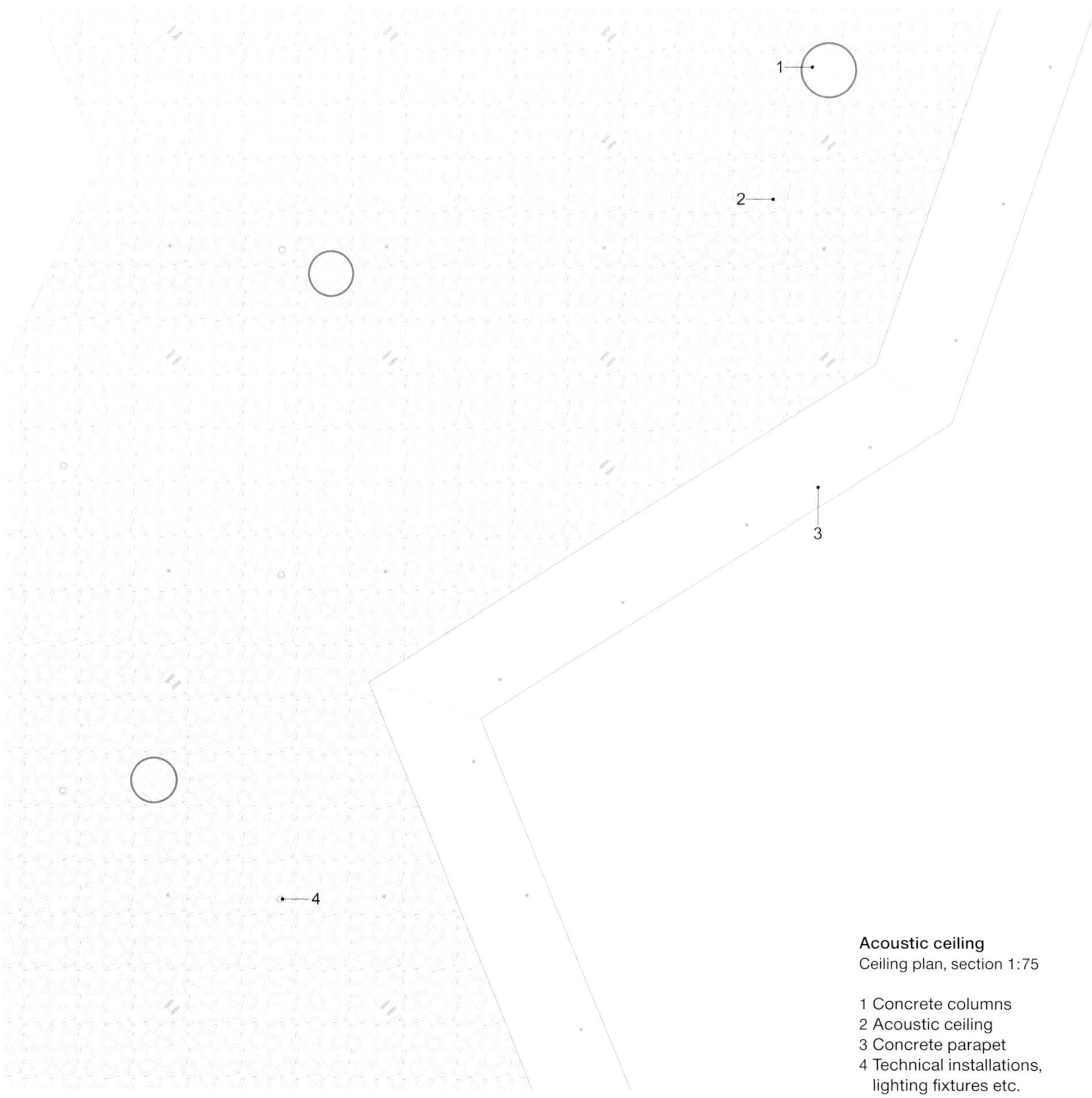

Acoustic ceiling
Ceiling plan, section 1:75

1 Concrete columns
2 Acoustic ceiling
3 Concrete parapet
4 Technical installations, lighting fixtures etc.

The Outer Shell

Another important element in achieving the building's environmental ambitions was the development of the volume and facade. The compact volume formed a good starting point for the creation of a building with low energy consumption, but it posed challenges in terms of providing good and even daylight throughout the deep building.

In the competition, the facade was conceived as an abstract curtain where the walls were filled with nanogel, a new insulation product that lets light through. In some places there would be larger openings with views that, in combination with smaller openings elsewhere, established contact with the surroundings. The one exception was at street level, where we wanted a completely transparent glass facade to make the transition between inside and outside more fluid so that the library space would be perceived as a continuation of the surrounding urban space.

Working models that show investigations of different directions in which the volume could develop.

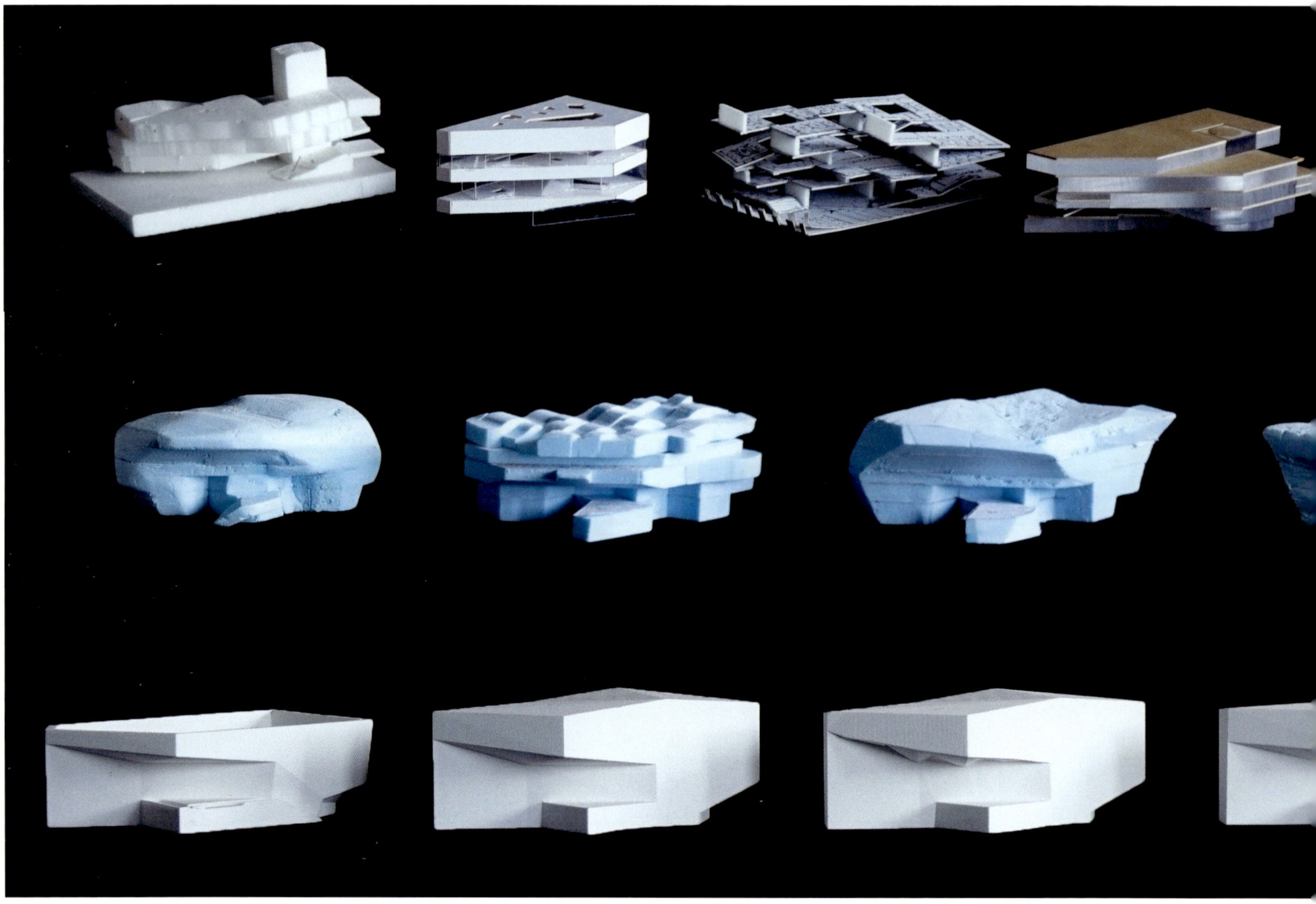

Early sketches of the geometry for the facade structure.

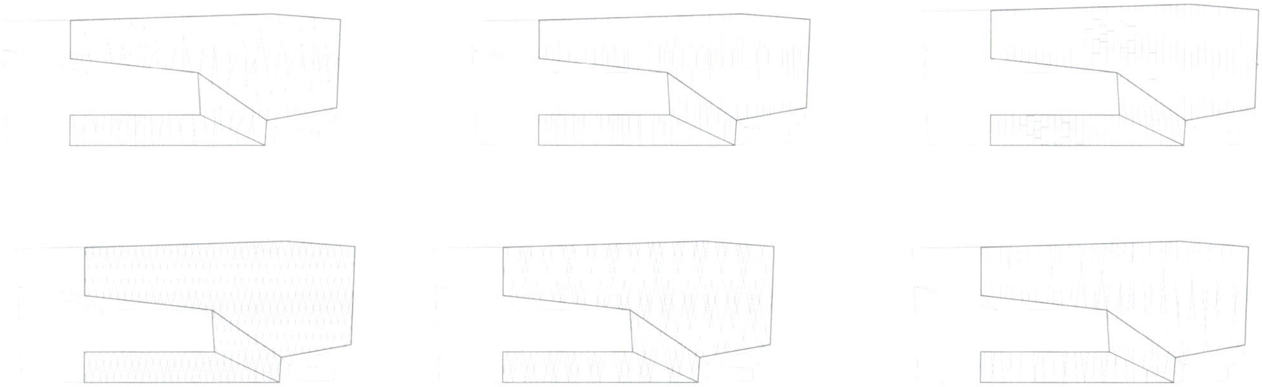

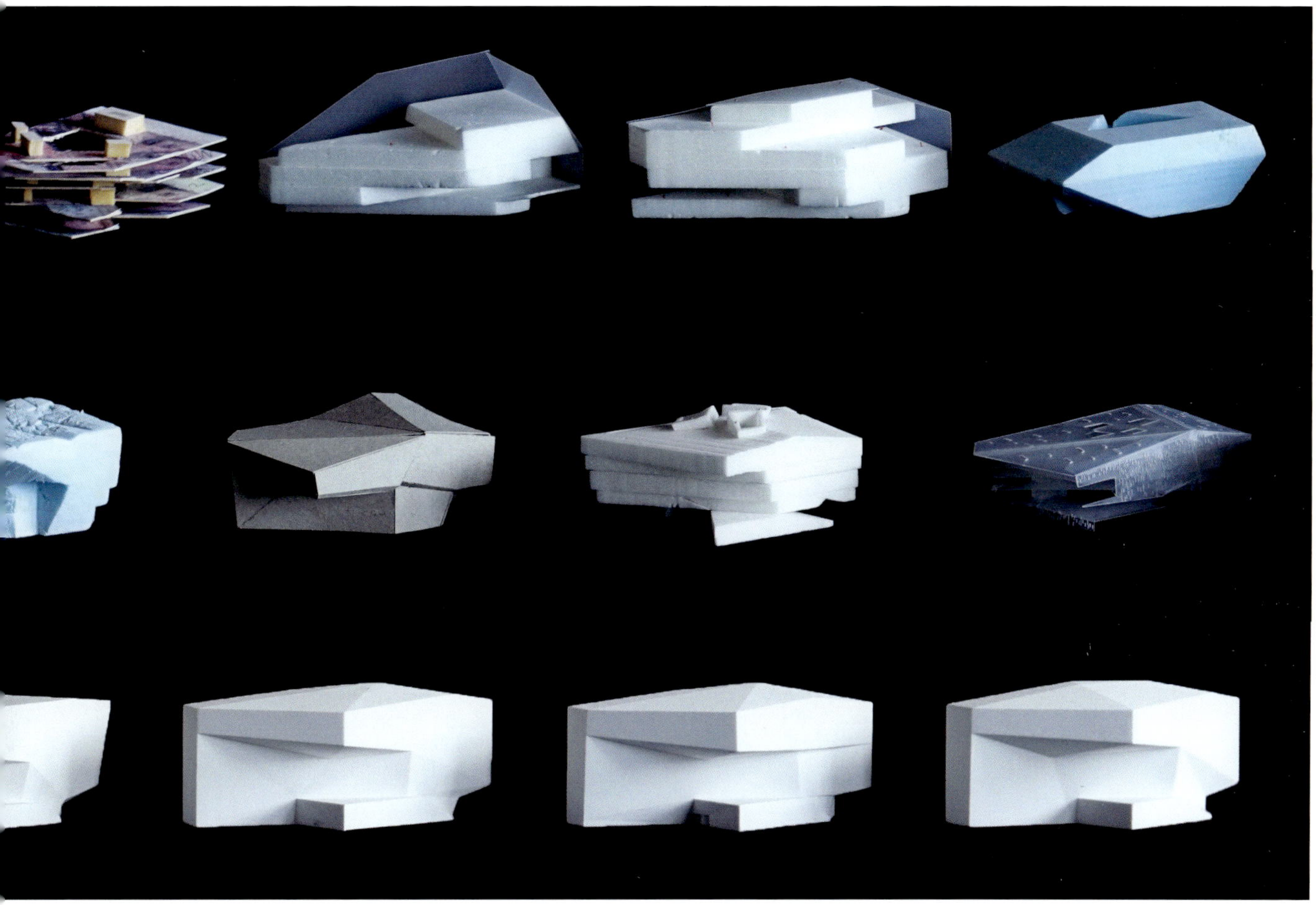

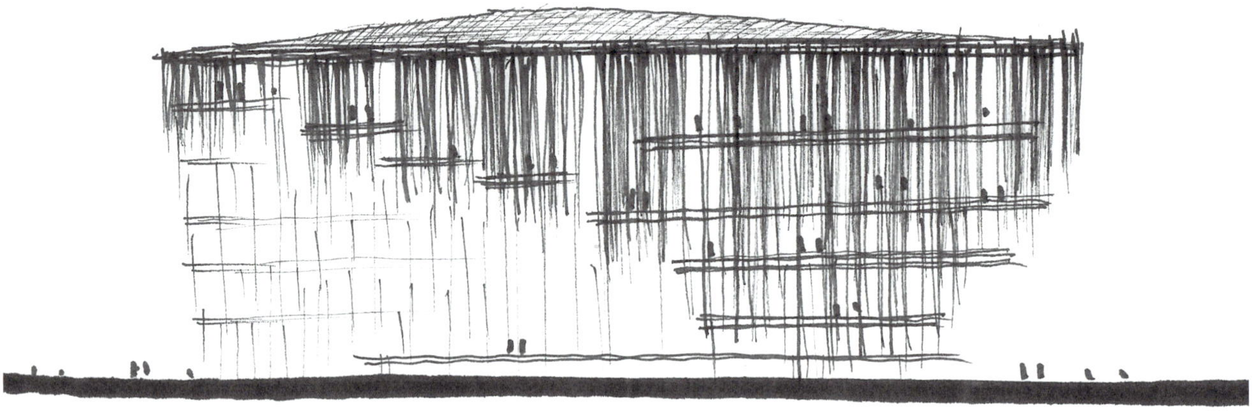

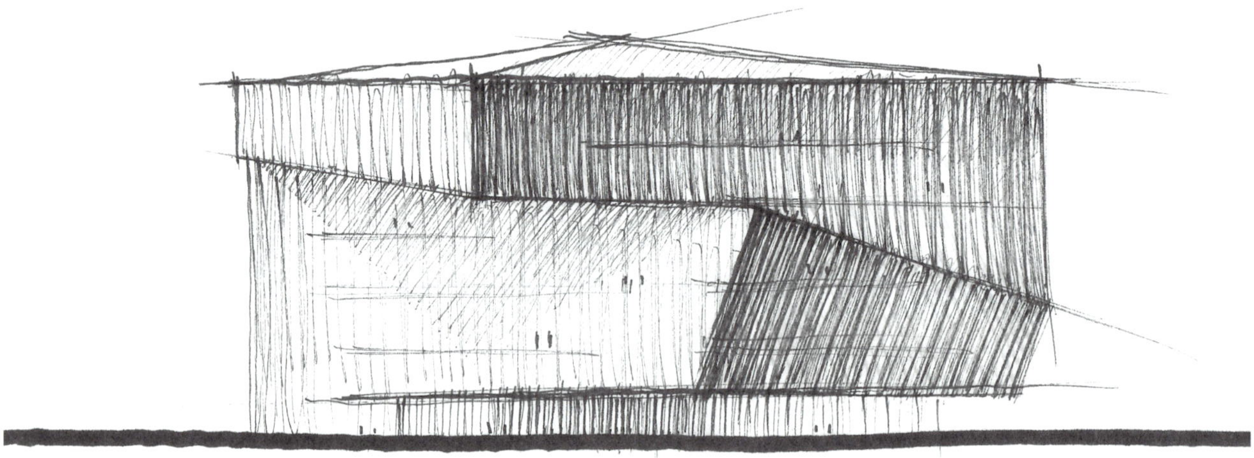

Sketches that investigate different principles for the development of volume and facade.

Should the volume be cultivated as a crystalline form or more like a hanging tree?

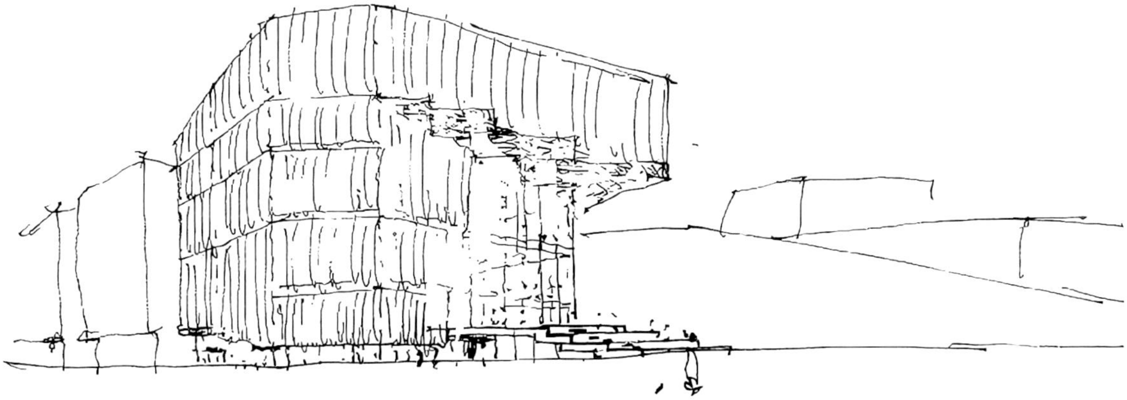

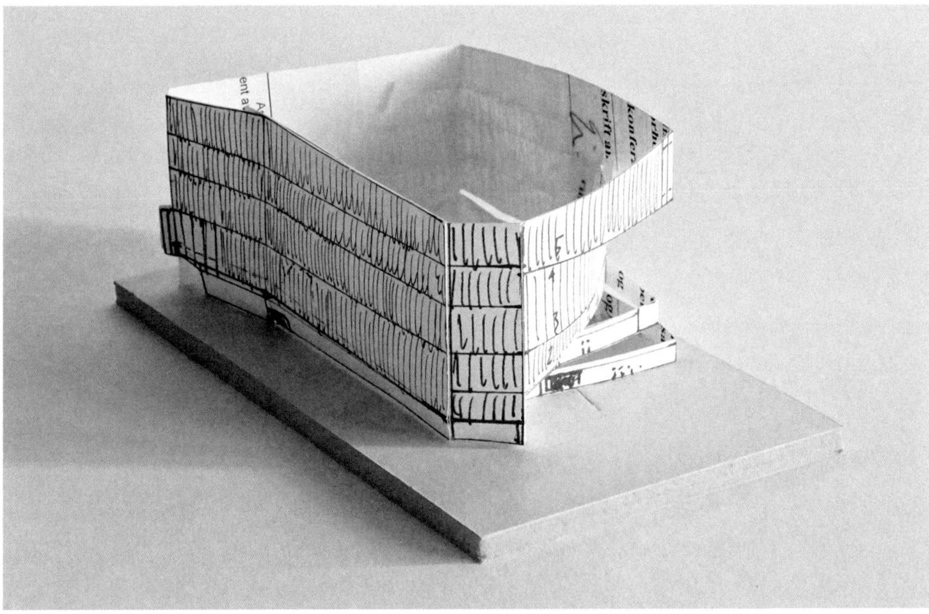

The volume developed away from a crystalline form to a structure where the various slabs were accentuated to break up the volume.

After the competition, the municipality specified and increased their environmental ambitions for the library. It was decided that the library should conform to passive house standards, requiring a minimum of 50 percent lower greenhouse gas emissions than similar buildings. They wanted the library to be the most energy-efficient cultural building in Norway. The project was also one of the first role model projects in FutureBuilt, an innovation arena where the role models are intended to extend well beyond current practice in the construction industry.

As a consequence of the heightened environmental ambitions, it was decided that the facade would have to consist of 50 percent closed insulated fields and only 50 percent glass areas with active sun protection. The latter was necessary to keep the solar heat out in the summer and utilize the heat and daylight in the winter. The nanogel panels had size limitations that made it difficult to meet the stricter requirements for heat loss, daylight, and sun protection. As there was also a requirement for external sun protection, that solution eventually became too expensive.

We wanted a facade that felt as light and open as the translucent curtain from the competition, but which also fulfilled the high environmental ambitions for the project. The solution was a facade structure with a rhythm that filters the light evenly throughout the facade.

Different model studies of the facade in 1:20 and 1:50. It was a challenge to achieve the evenly bright facade that we had envisaged in the competition's proposal, with large areas of the facade being closed. The solution was to distribute the closed areas evenly through the facade in combination with translucent glass that blurs out the shadows, to achieve the atmosphere we wanted for the interior.

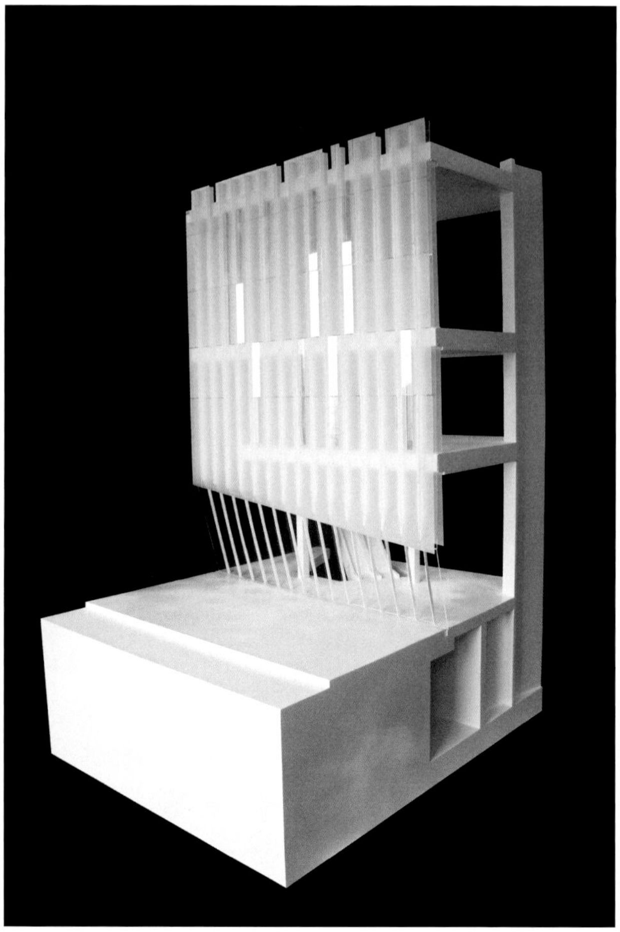

Custom-made fiberglass elements were designed as a prefabricated unit that combines facade structure, frame, and climate skin in one and the same element. This is a more production-efficient solution than a traditional facade, which is composed of a number of steel and aluminum parts, and the cold bridges in the facade construction are minimized. The elements have a curved cross section that reduces the shadows of the closed parts and lets as much light as possible into the library.

The facade system consists of two different elements, a standard element and a narrower element wich is used in the areas where the facade opens up to the view, the so-called oases. The composite elements also carry an inner and outer layer of glass. The inner layer consists of a matt satinato glass that spreads the light further into the building at the same time as it blurs the shadows further and creates a calm and light background for the interior. The outer layer shelters the sun protection from wind so that it can be used more days a year and contributes to higher insulation capacity against heat loss and external sound. This layer consists of a mixture of matte glass and ornamental glass with a texture, in addition to transparent glass in front of areas with a view. The variation means that the facade captures and reflects light in different ways, and the proportion of matte glass means that large reflections are avoided, which is otherwise common with glass facades.

The composite facade consists of two types. Facade type A1 has a larger closed area with internal glass and small openings. Facade type A2 are narrower elements without internal glass and are used in places with panoramic views (oases).

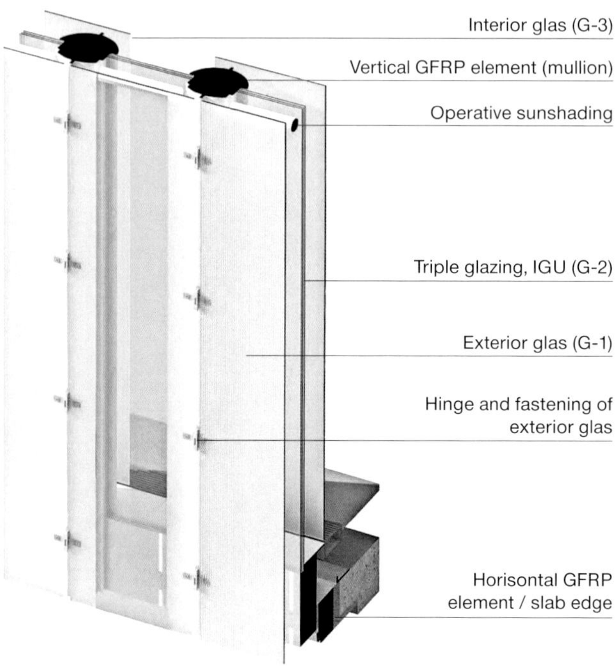

A1

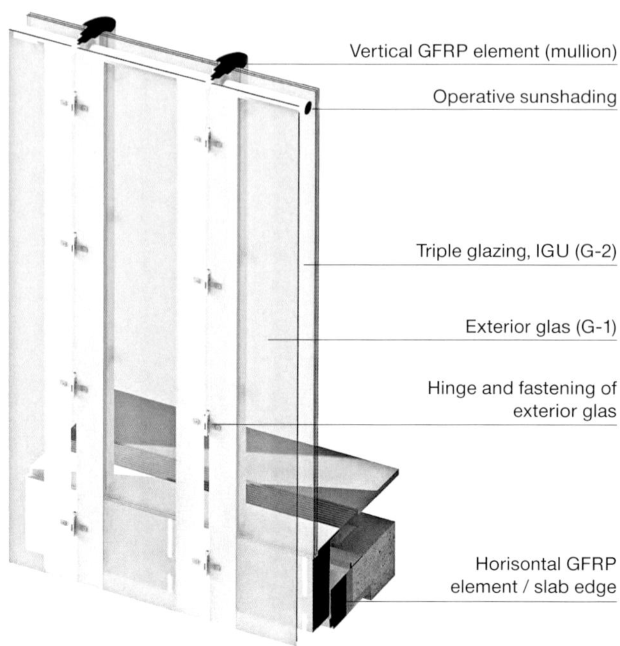

A2

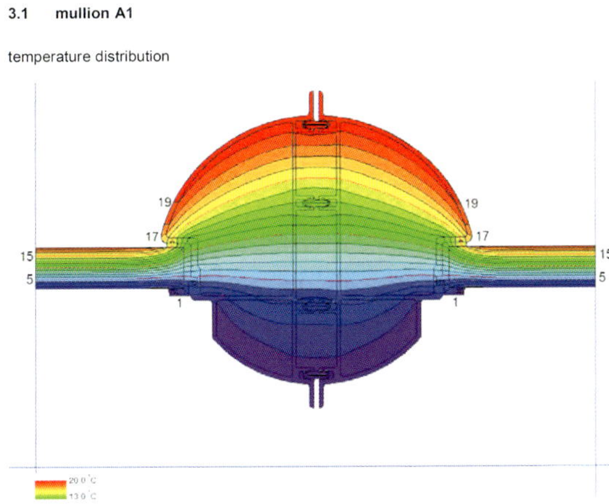

The composite elements are filled with rock wool. A number of U-value calculations had to be done along the way to ensure that the passive house requirements were met. (Illustration: Roschmann)

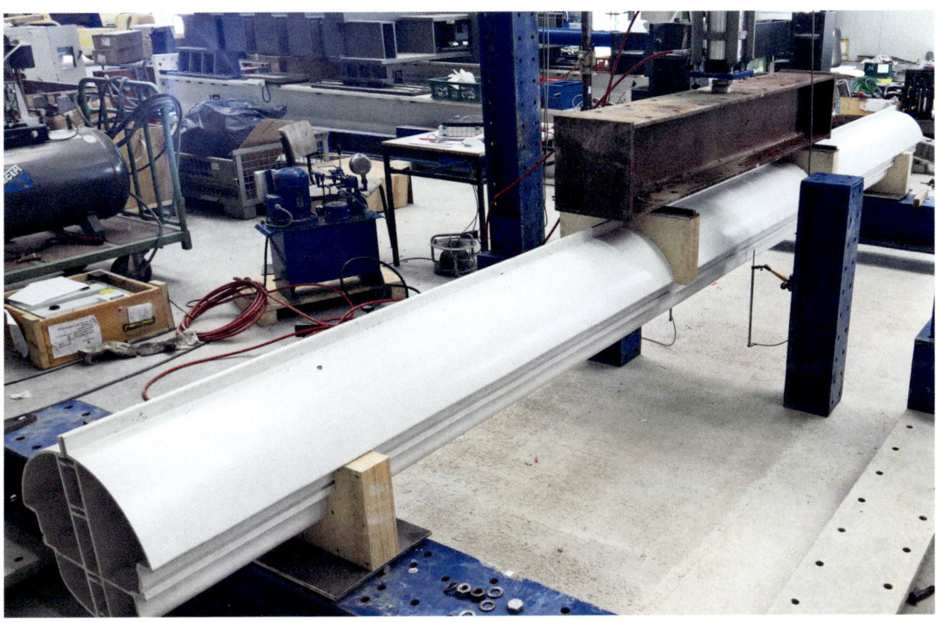

The facade elements had to undergo a series of tests to document that they met the requirements for strength, fire, etc. The facade handles spans up to 10.5 meters.

Form drawings of composite elements A1 and A2. The facade consists of a number of different elements that were pultruded.
(Illustration: Roschmann)

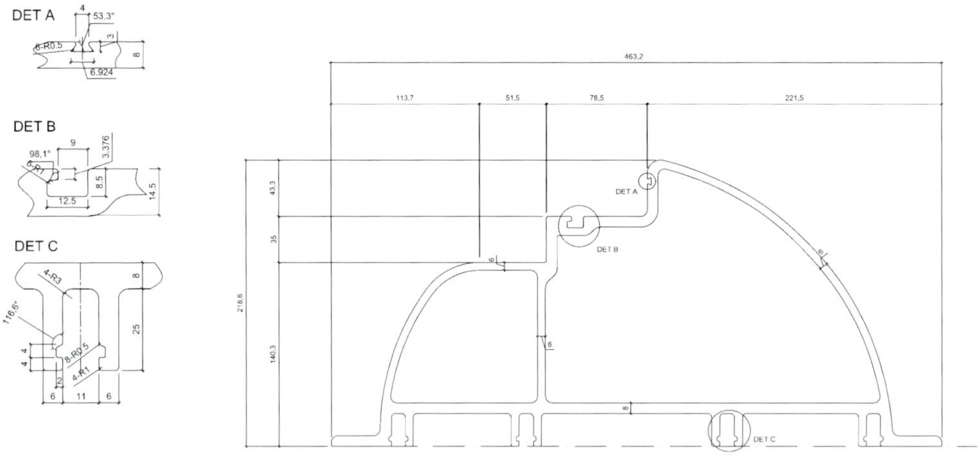

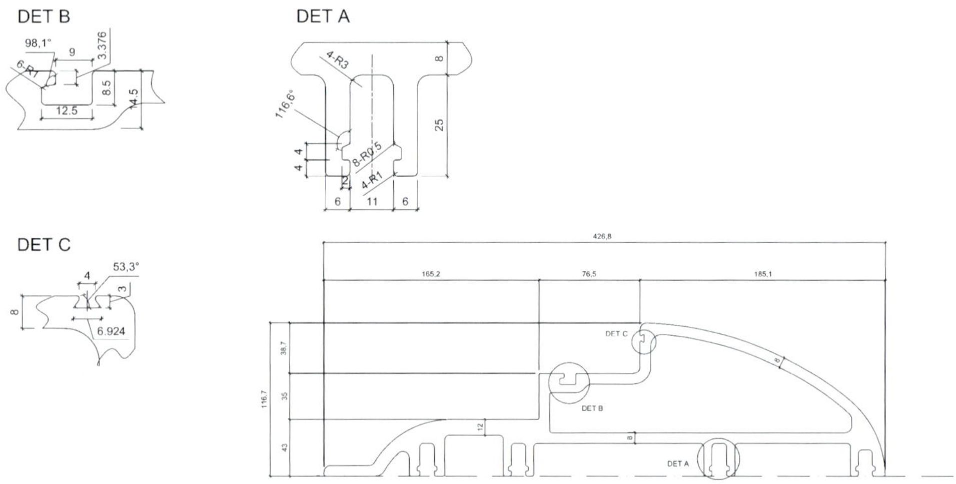

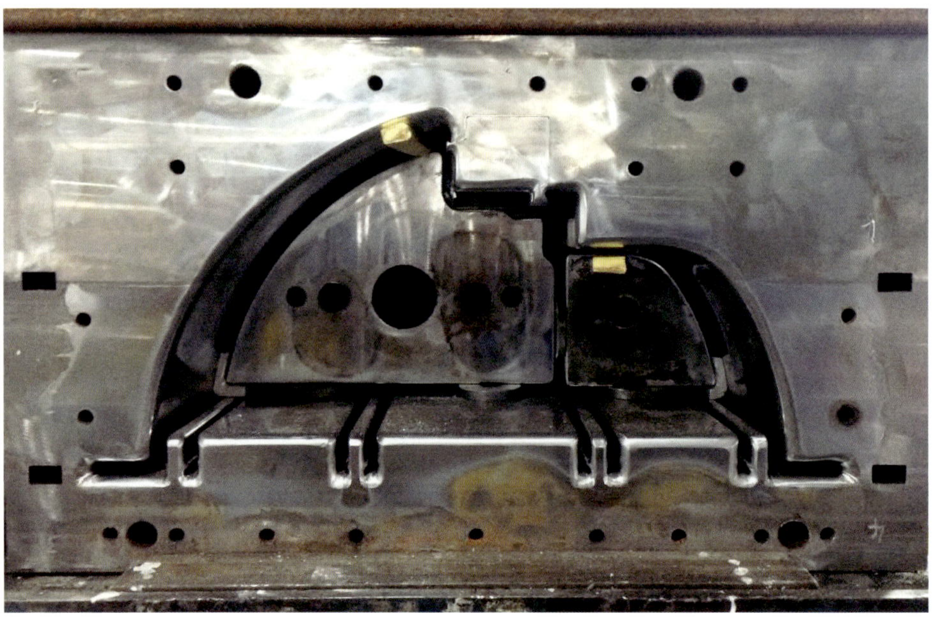

Mold for pultrusion of composite-element for facade type A1.

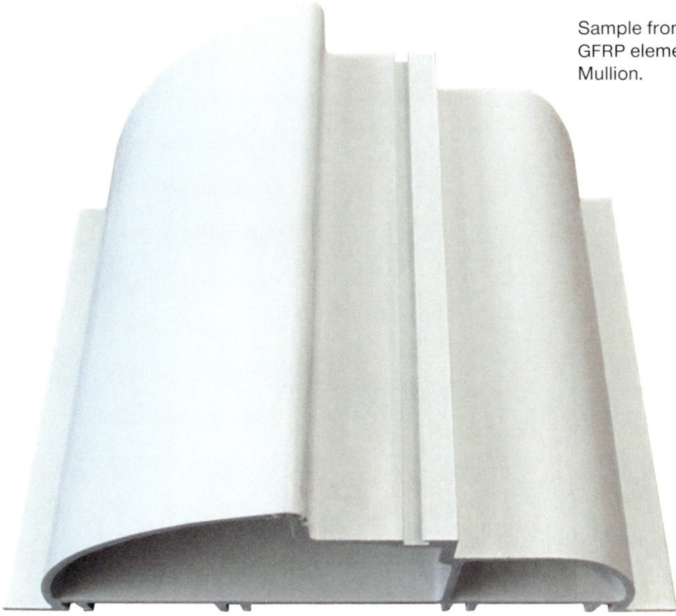

Sample from Roschmann of GFRP element for Facadetype A1 Mullion.

Images from inspection of a full-scale model at Roschmann's facility in Gersthofen.

Facade
Horizontal section 1:25

1 Facade type A1 mullion, GFRP element filled with mineral wool
2 Facade type A2 mullion, GFRP element filled with mineral wool
3 Triple glazing, IGU
4 Exterior glass (clear, satinato and ornamental glass), openable
5 Aluminum hinge
6 Guide rail for sun protection
7 Interior glass (satinato), openable
8 Steel profile for supporting the outer glass corner
9 Convector

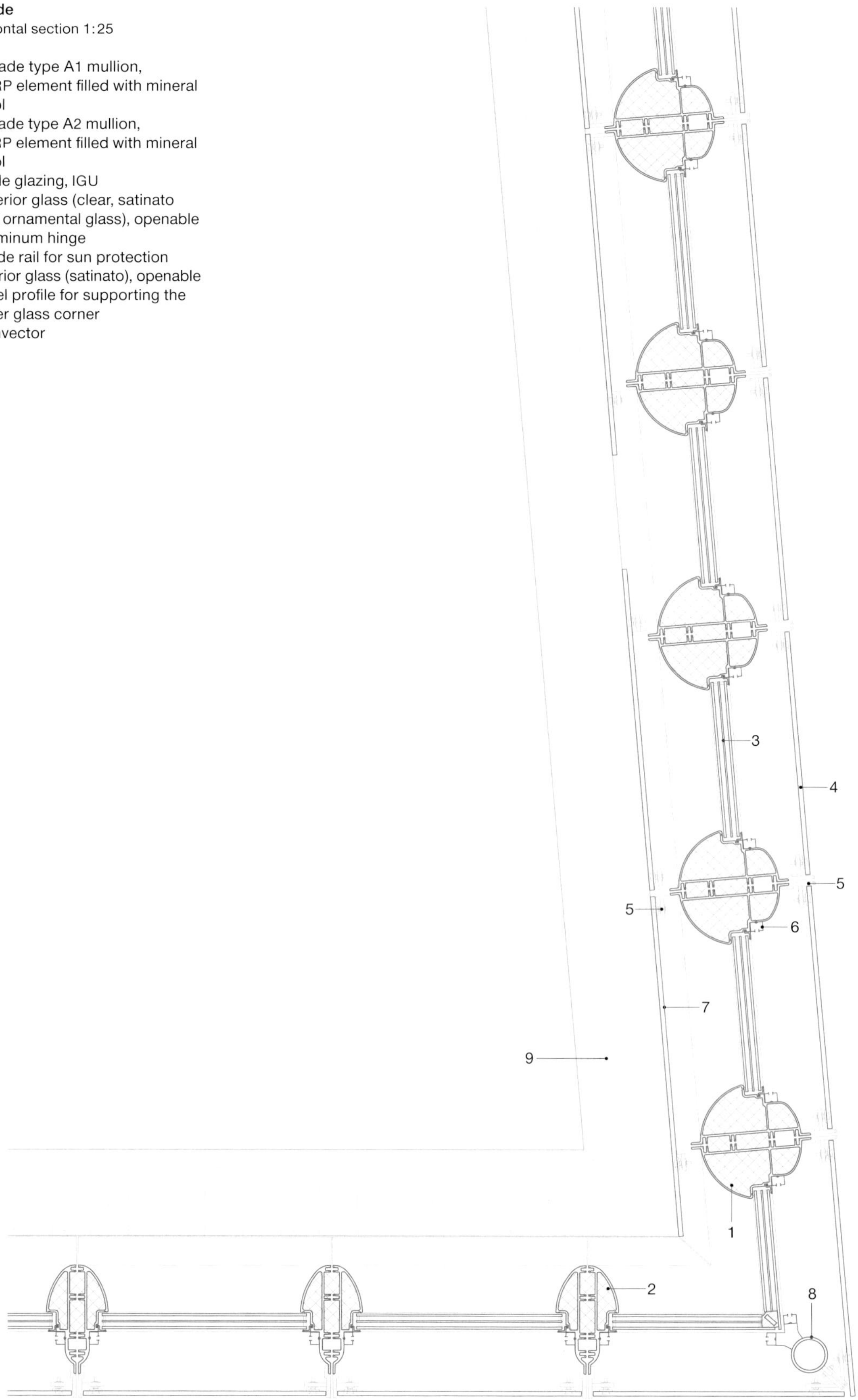

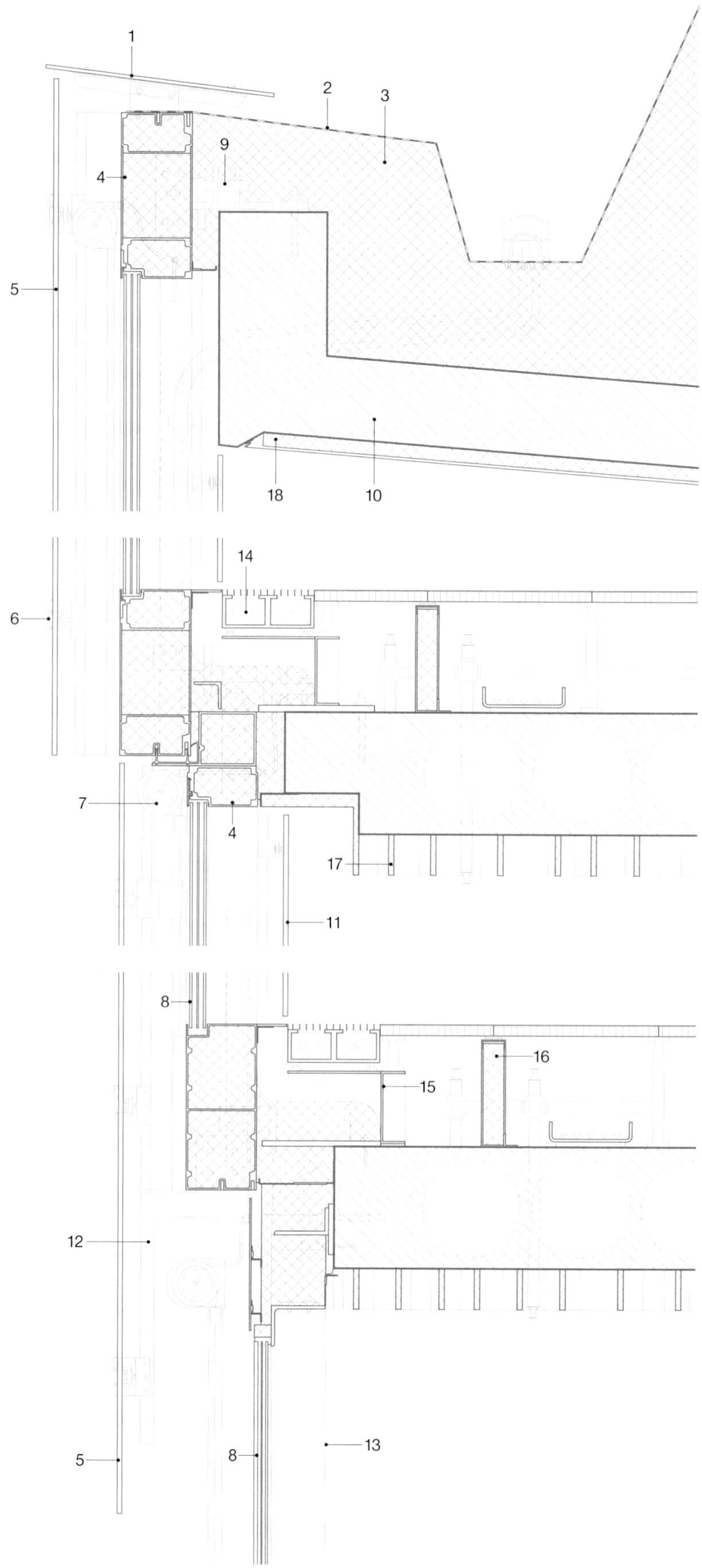

Facade
Detailed section 1:25

1 Glass cornice
2 Roof membrane, light gray
3 Insulation, mineral wool
4 GFRP element filled with mineral wool
5 Outer glass (clear, satinato and ornamental glass), openable
6 Aluminum hinge
7 Sun protection
8 Triple glazing, IGU
9 Bracket for hanging the facade onto the concrete slab
10 Concrete slab
11 Interior glass, satinato
12 Steel fin for supporting external glass
13 Steel profile for facade at street level
14 Convector
15 Bracket for installation floor and convector
16 Wall for closure of air chamber / raised floor
17 Acoustic baffle ceiling
18 Recessed acoustic ceiling, "stretch ceiling"

The Content of Deichman Bjørvika Is Developed

A program for a building project usually defines overall goals for the client and general requirements and needs related to function and quality. Along with a detailed list of all functions and rooms, their space requirements, functional requirements and so on are listed. Ordinarily, a detailed room and function program is prepared in advance, before an architectural competition is announced. It was thus quite unusual that the functional program for the new library in Bjørvika was more general and conceptual. The overall goal of the competition was to create a new library designed "based on user movements and patterns in conjunction with the library's facilities and services."

The new building was to be an open cultural and knowledge arena structured "on the users' needs for services rather than on the collection and should challenge traditional perceptions of how a library works."

The program was split between internal administration areas and audience areas divided into four subgroups: general audience areas, information center, 24-hour library, auditorium and cinema. The description of general public areas contained reading areas for the public, media collections, self-service, reception, café / canteen, meeting rooms, copy and print center, cloakroom and toilets. There was no specification of what activities we were to facilitate within this general public area.

In the phase we were now entering, the functional program had to be specified in more detail. What activities would take place in this building? What kind of requirements did these activities place on space, equipment, acoustics, and technology? What activities could take place outside in the large continuous library space, and what activities needed more specialized, closed rooms? How to prioritize? How to create a completely new library typology?

In the competition program, it was stated that the new main library should:

- *play a leading role in the development of the modern public libraries*
- *be an important source of knowledge and culture to the general public*
- *reach new user groups through new technology*
- *be a meeting point for sharing experience, debate and cultural diversity*
- *create broad awareness of literature and be a learning resource that will stimulate both the love of reading and literary insight*
- *consolidate Oslo as an international and multicultural capital.*

Working models were essential for librarians and architects to be able to discuss spatial solutions and opportunities. Around the model, one could work on developing the program and the building together.

In the aftermath of the competition a great deal of work was done by the library to develop a first draft for distribution and detailing of the space program, based on the architectural concept from the competition. The further development of the program then took place through a close collaboration between librarians, architects – and later the interior architects.

This parallel development of the program and the building constituted a very rare opportunity where the spatial structure had the potential to affect the development of the program and the distribution of functions and vice versa. We believe that the fact that we had time for such a process made it possible to respond to the ambitions of the competition to develop the modern public library and create a whole new library typology.

This also corresponds well with former library manager Liv Sæteren's description of how to create a new library typology:

"When the libraries now have to be changed drastically because the media landscape and working methods have changed – the library as client and the architect must be part of a creative process and create a new typology together."

The librarians had great knowledge and experience as to how a traditional library worked, but they were aware that what they were now looking for was something else, and they had no real references to what this new library could be.

Our collaboration was exciting and fruitful. The librarians had many ideas and thoughts about activities and services they wanted in the library, but they needed help to explore the spatial requirements and consequences. We also had many interesting discussions and studies related to the relationship between functions. How open could the library actually be? The acoustic conditions grew important. Nobody wanted a traditional library where everyone had to be quiet. We needed an informal atmosphere where people could meet and work together, and where activities such as reading, debates or events could simultaneously take place in the open library space. But did that imply that the library would be perceived as noisy? Would it be impossible to sit and concentrate?

A number of acoustic measures were incorporated into the project. With the help of the acoustic engineers, we created a digital model where you could stroll through the building and experience simulations of how sound was distributed to the different areas. Eventually we became confident that the building could handle a number of parallel activities in the open library area. (Fortunately, this has been confirmed after the building was taken into use by Oslo's residents.)

Sketch model from 2011 with the first attempt to lay out the functional program.

First overview of the distribution of the program for the public areas, December 2011. (Illustration: Deichman)

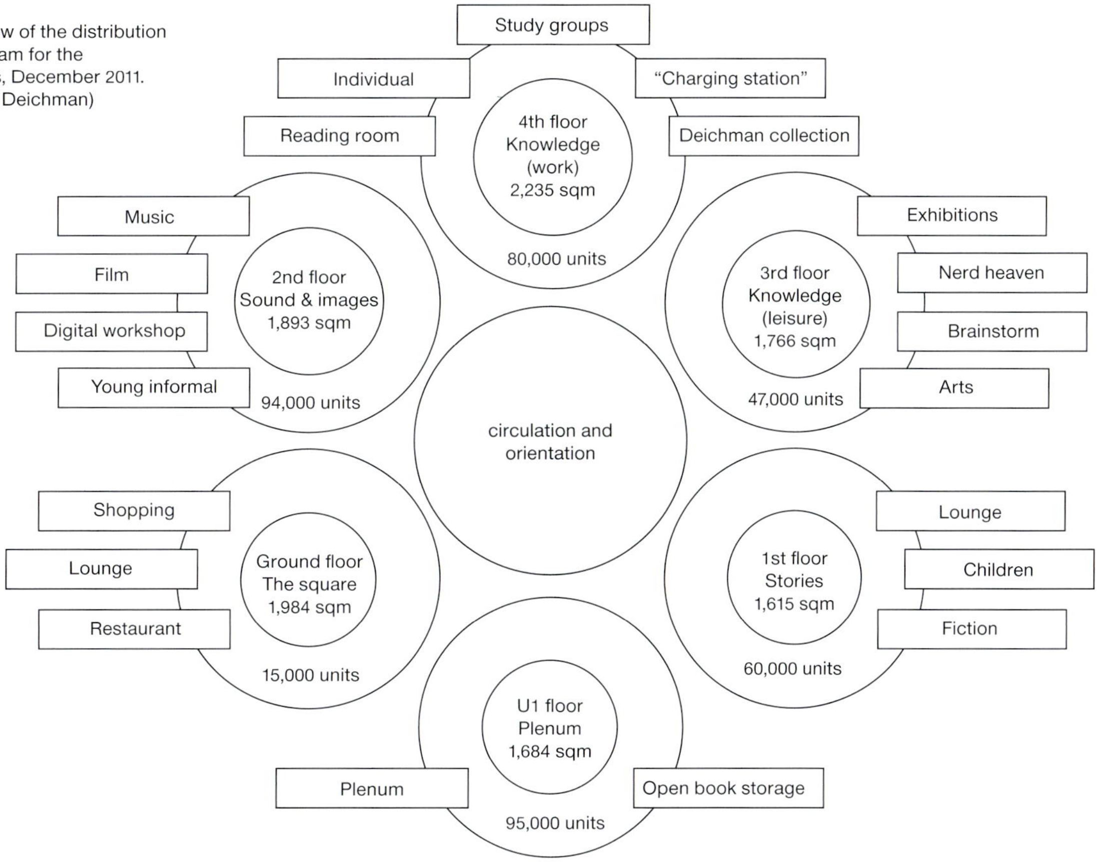

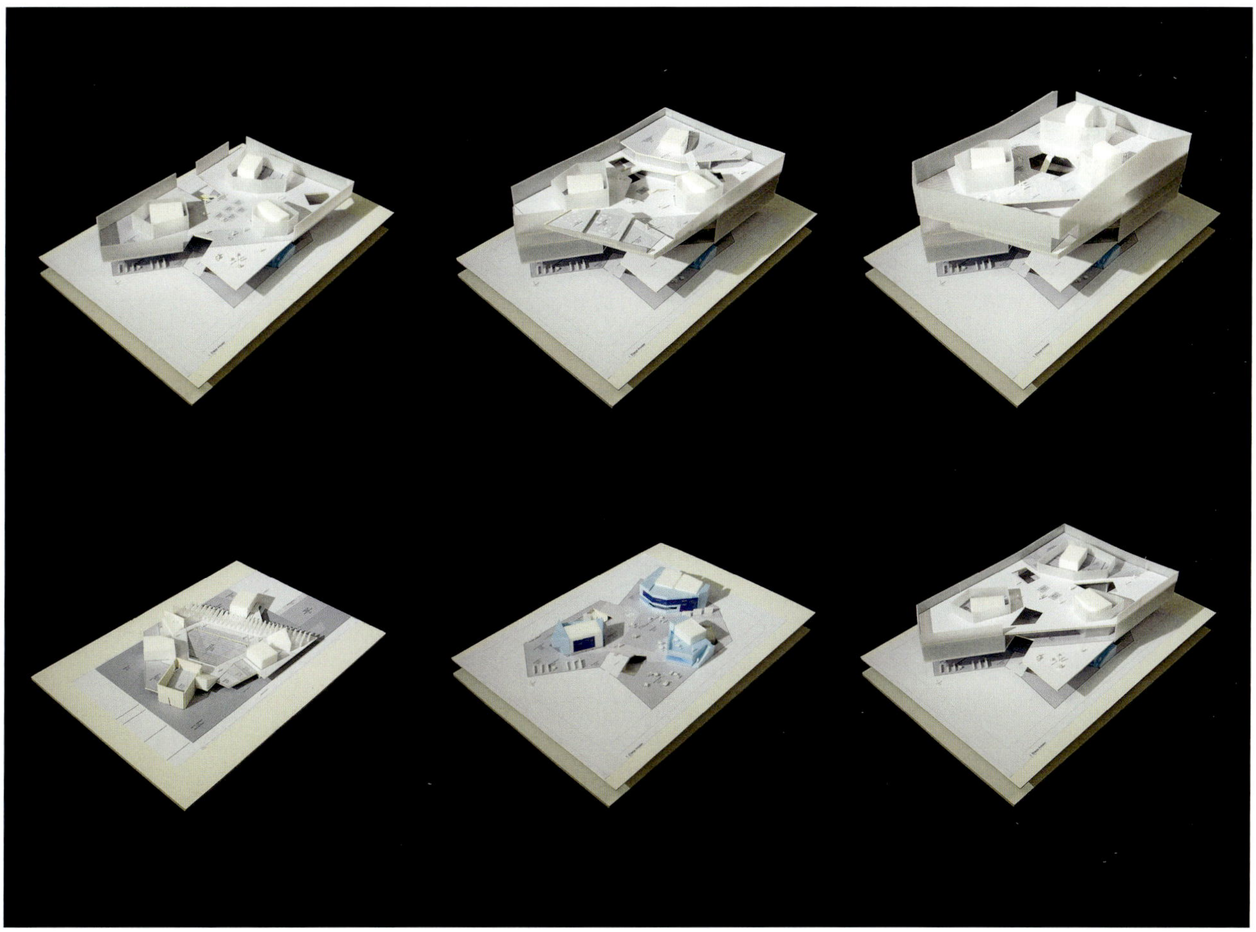

The Shining Cores – Rooms and Niches as Varied and Exotic Environments

The competition's four light shafts were eventually reduced to three, and then it fit naturally into the structure to have three technical cores between these, which could accommodate all technical infrastructure that requires vertical continuity, such as lifts and escape stairs. In communion with the light shafts, these three technical cores define the building's spatial structure. At the same time, they have an important bracing function for the main structure.

As the functional program of the library was developed, one also saw the need for a series of special rooms of different sizes, which would serve as context for the rich offerings the librarians wanted the building to have. These rooms were organized around the technical cores with niches that could form exhibition areas for current topics. On the three floors with higher ceiling heights (ground, second, fourth) there was room for mezzanines above these areas, offering more secluded places for the users of the library.

This spatial organization means that the facades can be kept free and allow daylight to flow in from all sides. The outermost layer around the the three cores are clad with shelves – or a media rack – in raw steel from floor to ceiling. As such they form three freestanding book towers with functions

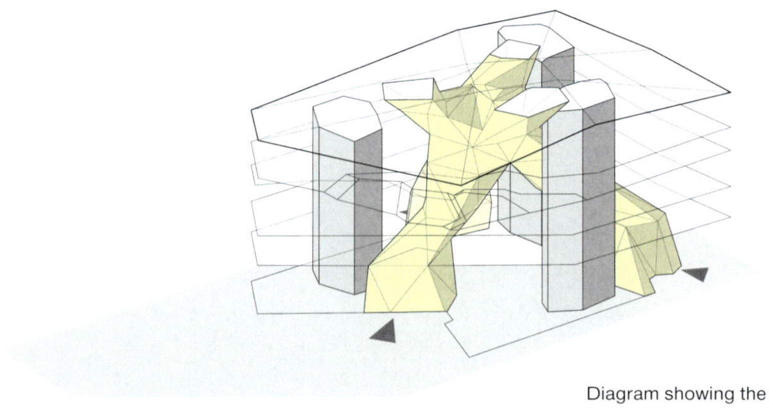

Diagram showing the three technical cores placed between the three light shafts.

Study model 1:25 of the relationship between niches and small rooms and the open library space.

that support and complement the open, continuous library space, which extends from the lower floor to the top.

These book towers establish different zones on each level and allow for free movement along the facades without dead ends. This is a spatial organization that inspires wandering and exploration. Together with the light shafts that create connections between the floors, the towers corresponded well to the librarians' desire for openness and flexibility divided into zones – rooms in the room where informal events could be carried out.

Rooms and niches around the three cores gradually became important elements in our answer to what the future library should be. Here, visitors would find functions such as small meeting rooms, group rooms, games rooms, playrooms, cinemas, reading rooms, workshops and sound studios, developed in a close dialogue between librarians, interior architect and architects. The ambition is that the visitors not only come and borrow and use different media, but also produce their own content.

Sketch of the in-between space, the open library space around the cores.

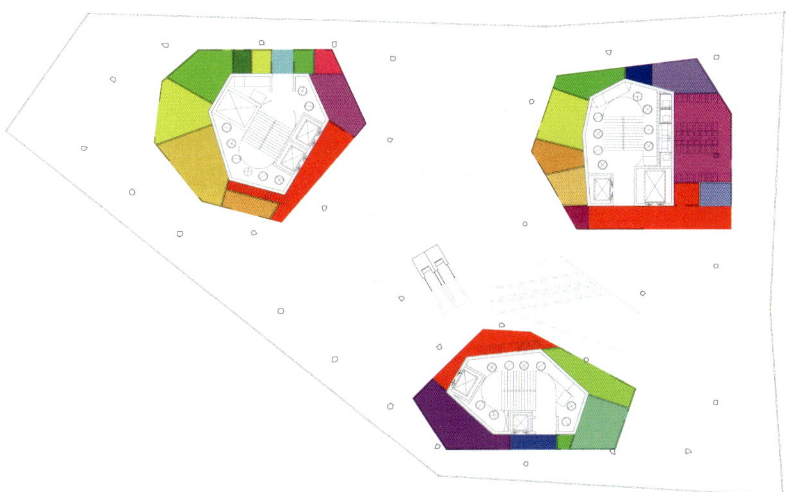

Diagram showing the strategy with the special rooms around the cores which contains a variety of functions and atmospheres.

Section diagram showing the three book towers with special rooms and different atmospheres; the open room in the middle, where the light shafts meet; and the large auditorium downstairs.

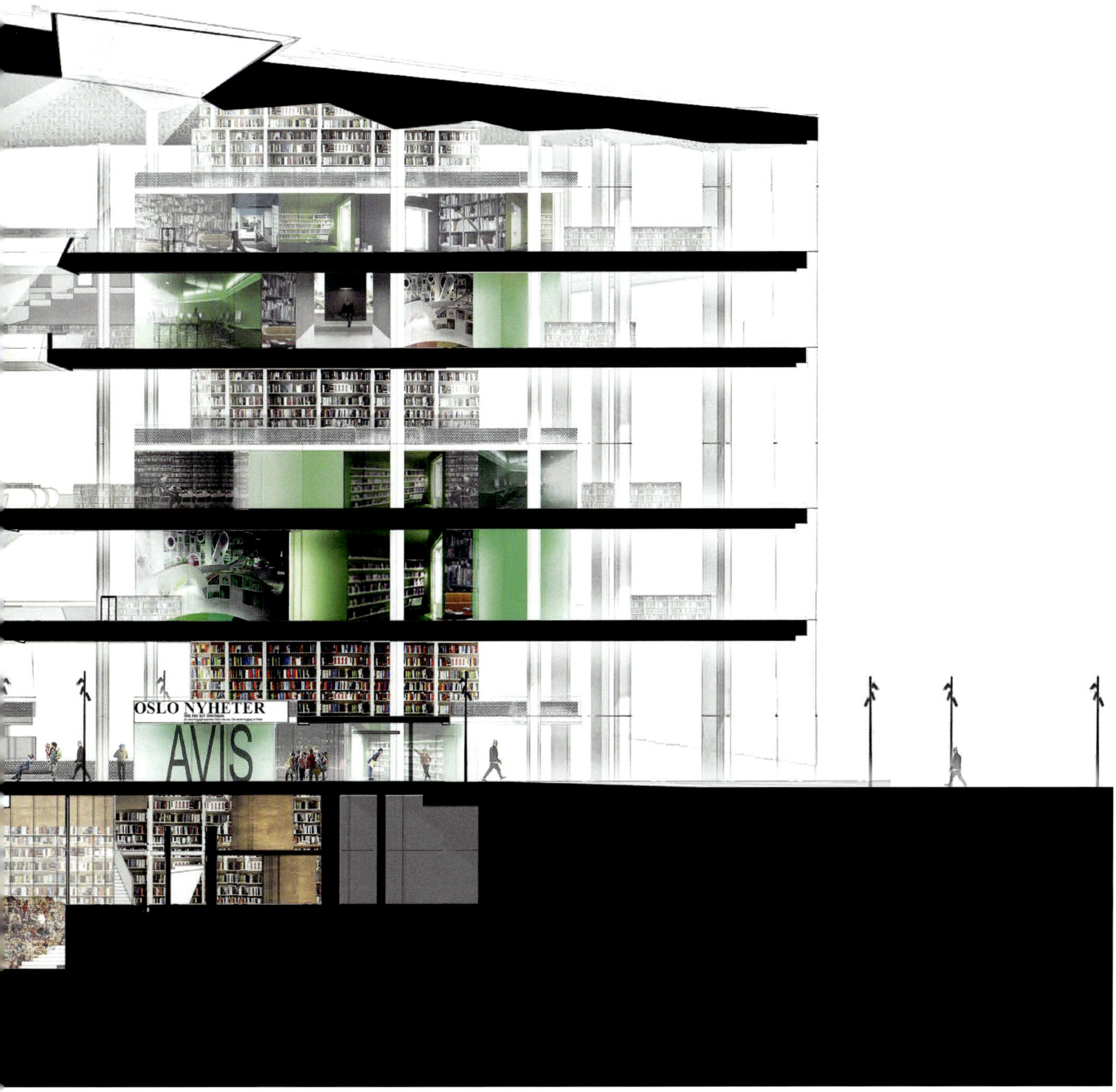
OSLO NYHETER
AVIS

The special rooms and niches were developed in close collaboration between librarians, interior architects and architects. We wanted these areas to be spaces where one could work freely and in varied ways, which would realize the library's ambition for a diversity of atmospheres.

The structuring of rooms and niches around the three book towers therefore combines the experience of a continuous library space and that of colorful and varied rooms and niches that reveal themselves as you move around the cores. The interior architects were given free rein to create diversity within these limited areas, which can also be easily changed according to future needs. The niches open up toward the library room and can serve as scenographic support for activities in the main room. They can accommodate temporary exhibitions where librarians curate and display parts of the library's content or focus on current topics.

The outermost layer around the cores with the media rack – "the new bookshelf" – extends from floor to ceiling. Many of the librarians thought walls lined with bookshelves were too traditional. In the development of this element we therefore had to define it as something more than an ordinary bookshelf. The bookshelf has become a flexible multifunctional wall, where you can hook off shelf plates and mount screens, exhibitions, information stations, etc. In addition to regular shelves, there are mounts, exhibition solutions, and various integrated screens that are adapted to the system. Everything is based on a specially developed system in which you can easily move the components around – and where new components can be made in the future.

The media rack system, stairs, railings, and wall coverings around the three cores are all produced in hot-rolled crude steel, a material with its own natural play and variety, and which patinates and turns finer with usage and time.

Example of a niche facing the open library space with the media rack around as the outer layer. From the children's department on the first floor.

Drawing showing examples of the various components that can be inserted in the media stand.

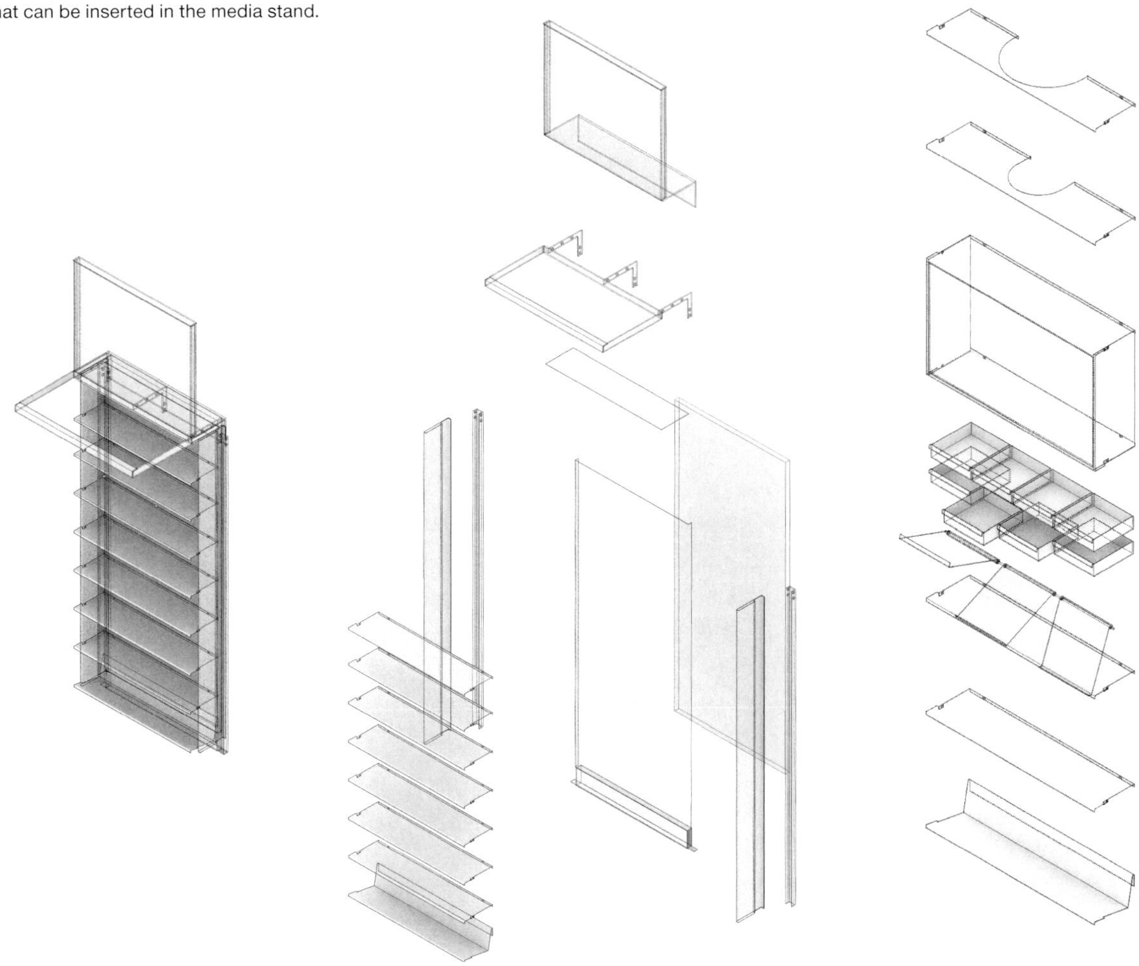

Illustrations of the media rack with stair up to the mezzanine level. All were later produced in hot-rolled crude steel.

Around the core in the northeast, the administration areas are located on all levels except the first floor. In this core you also find the book lift for the book sorting machine, which is the brain in the distribution of media in the new library. A large sorting machine in the basement sorts and spreads delivered media to the correct trolley on each floor. This sorting facility enables librarians to spend time with the users of the library instead of sorting and transporting books and is thus an essential prerequisite for the new library to be able to maintain such a wonderful offer to its users.

Traditionally, a large technical room for ventilation systems and so forth tends to be centralized in the basement or at the top of the building. The

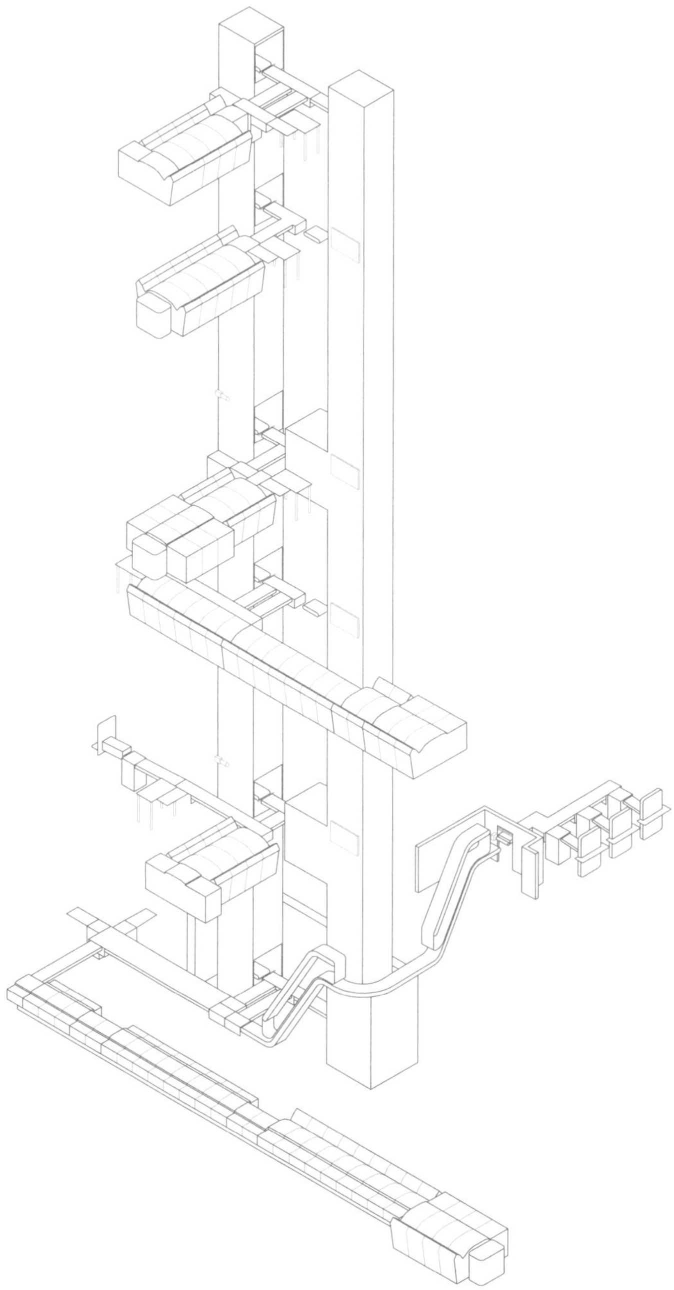

Illustration of the book sorting machine provided by Lyngsø. The facility connects all floors with the large sorting facility in the basement in addition to the 24-hour library and hand-in vending machines for book returns on the ground floor.

demanding ground conditions in Bjørvika eventually forced us to remove the lower ground floor where the technical rooms originally were to be located. This was a critical point in the process, but the solution we came up with was a decentralized ventilation system with the technical areas distributed In the three cores on the different floors.

A system with smaller units scattered around the building reduces the need for ventilation ducts and requires less energy to distribute the air in the building. The solution thus saves space as well as energy. In the beginning, however, we encountered problems with the ventilation rooms, which had to be placed on all levels, as they took up too much valuable library space. The solution was to place them on the mezzanine levels in the cores, freeing the areas below for larger special rooms connected to the open library areas.

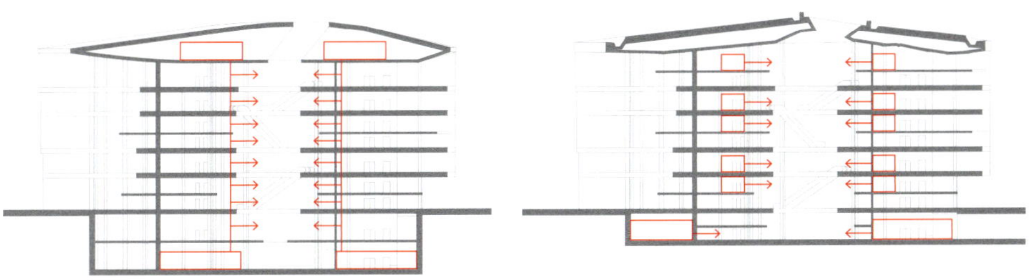

Diagram showing the switch from a centralized to a decentralized solution for the ventilation systems with reduced technical areas in the basement and technical attic.

Image from the building site showing the construction of the cores. These were cast with sliding formworks and erected in less than 10 days.

The building as a machine. Visualization of the BIM model showing the building's technical infrastructure.

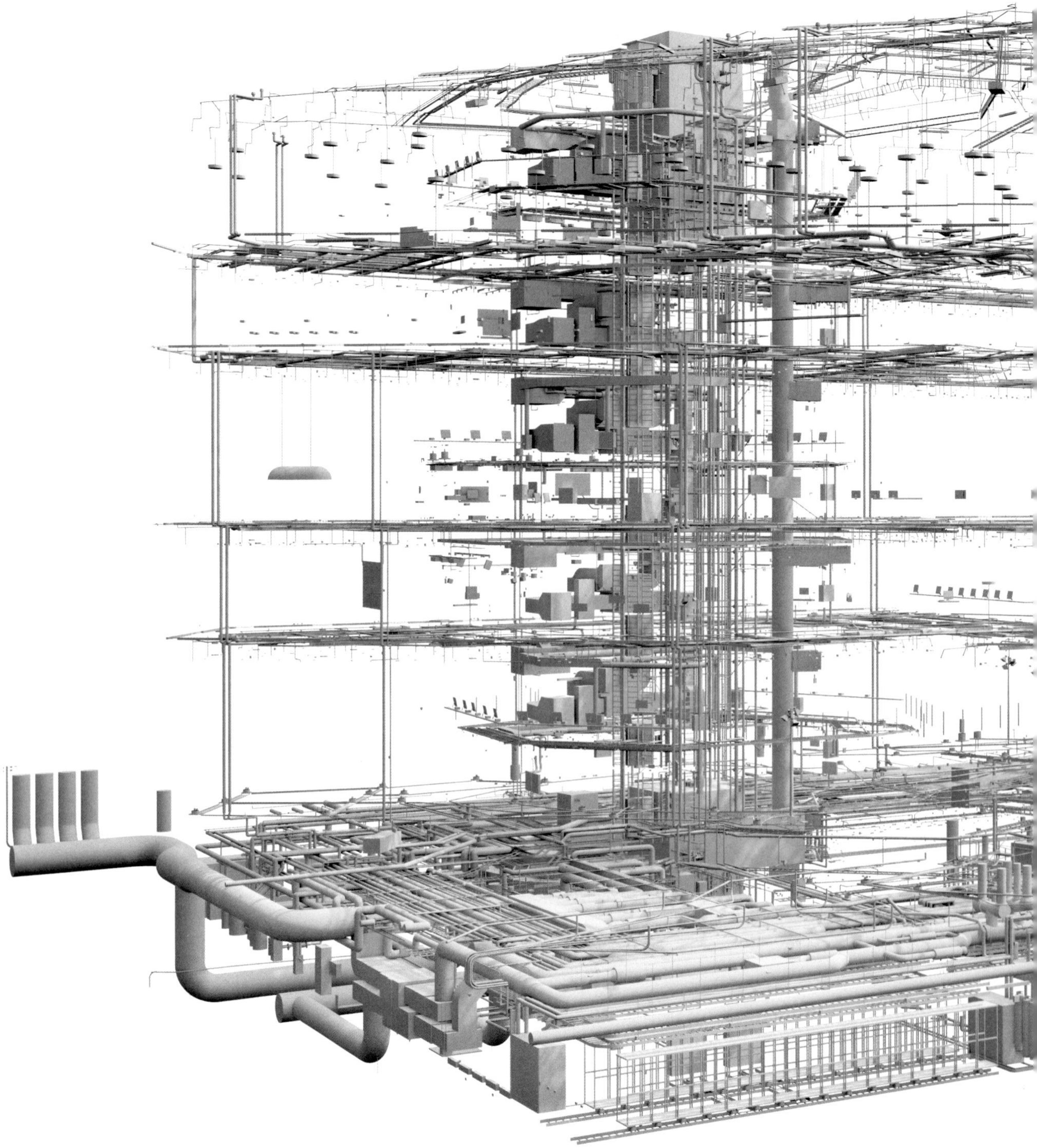

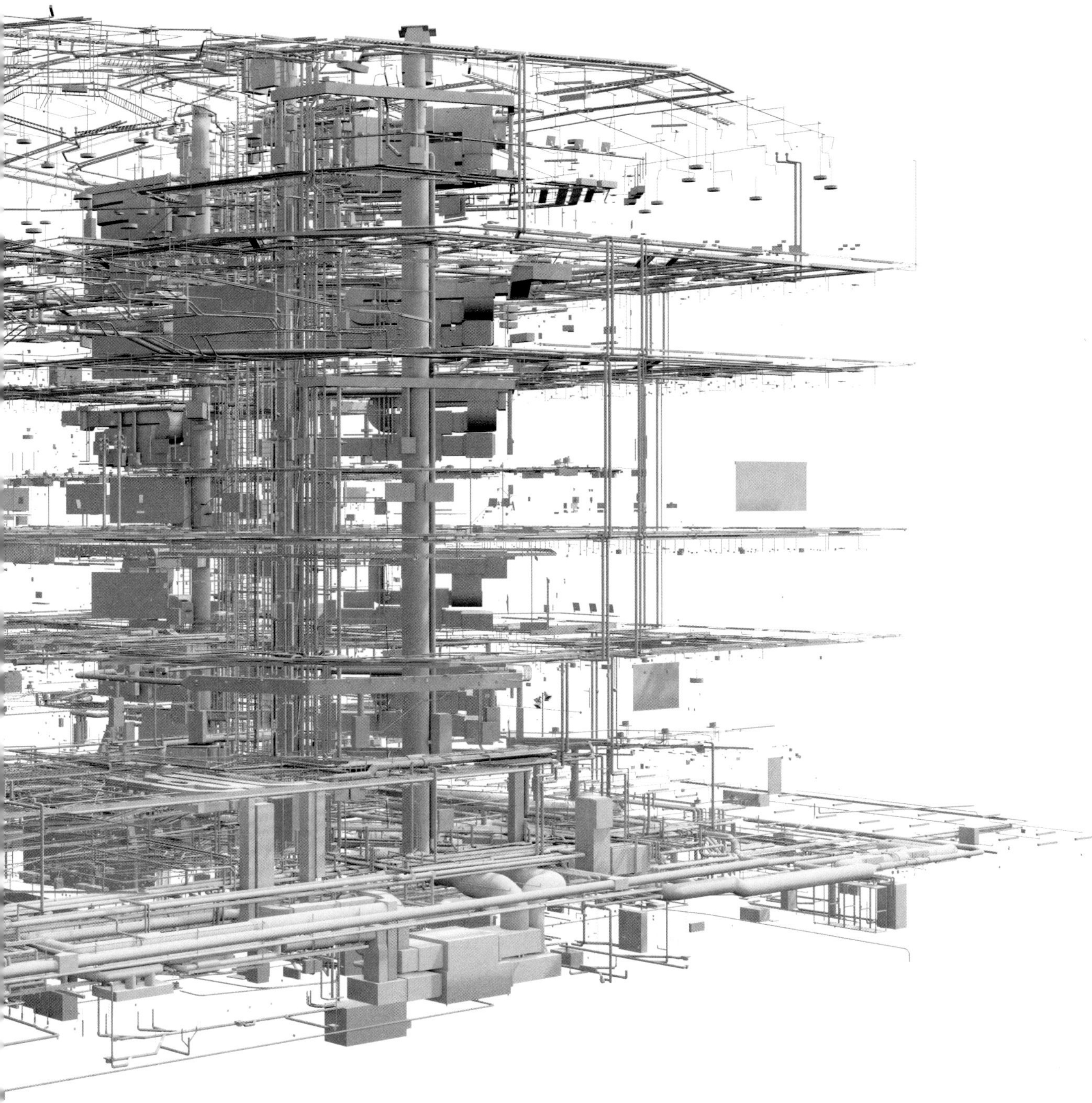

Plan 2nd floor. Working drawing showing all functions organized around the three cores.

2200
4000
E
D2
D1
D
C2
C1
C
B2
B1
B
A2
A1
A
TYPISK TRAPP RØYKAVKAST
2100
2001
2200

Media stand and mezzanine
Detailed section 1:25

1 Railings, perforated hot-rolled steel
2 Worktable, hot-rolled steel with linoleum top
3 Concrete slab for mezzanine
4 Lighting, integrated in hot-rolled steel profile
5 Perforated steel plate with acoustic absorption behind
6 Media rack, hot rolled steel
7 Stairs, hot-rolled steel
8 Electrical ducts
9 Structure for raised floor
10 Sprinkler system
11 Air chamber for ventilation

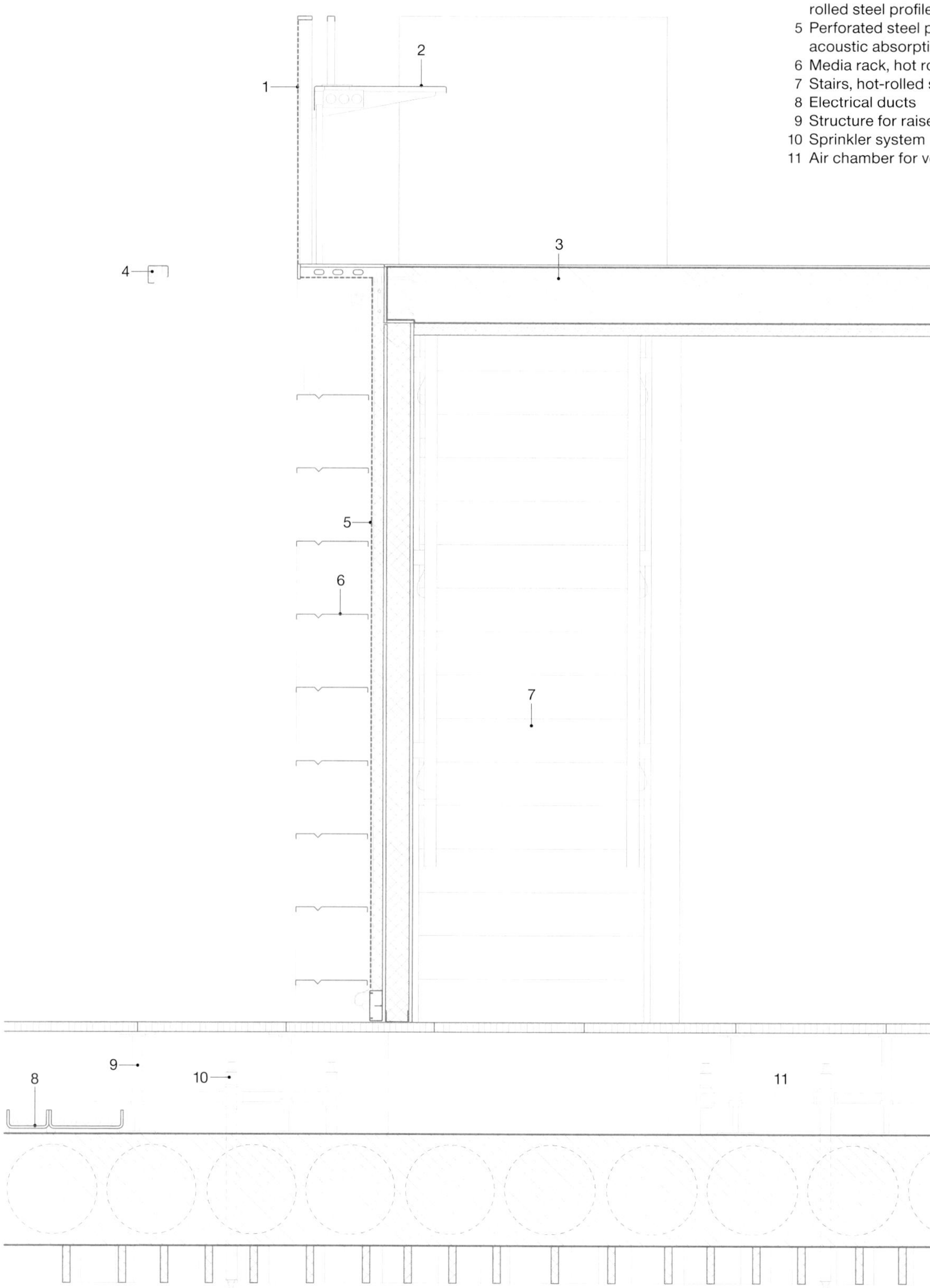

3M
MUSIKK - NOTER
Sheet Music
Studie 3.1 - 3.2
Musikk
Music
3M
MUSIKK - NOTER
Sheet Music
Noter
Sheet Music

Freestanding Furniture

In 2010, Scenario interior architects won the assignment announced by the City of Oslo for "interior architect services for the new Deichman main library." The assignment included freestanding furniture and user equipment. This initiated a close and good collaboration between the librarians, the interior architects and the architects on the design of the interior of the library. In the planning of the freestanding furniture, important considerations were the definition of the various departments and guidance of visitors. Each zone has a unique scenography that is emphasized by furniture choices and space-built interior elements. To create a consistent element that would link the various departments together, Scenario also designed a separate chair for the project, the "Deichman chair." The chair combines the desire for a visual link with the need for a good work chair.

The freestanding furniture is important for creating varied zones in the large contiguous library space.

Drawing of the “Deichman chair” by Scenario interior architects.
Below you see an image of the chair next to one of the light shafts.

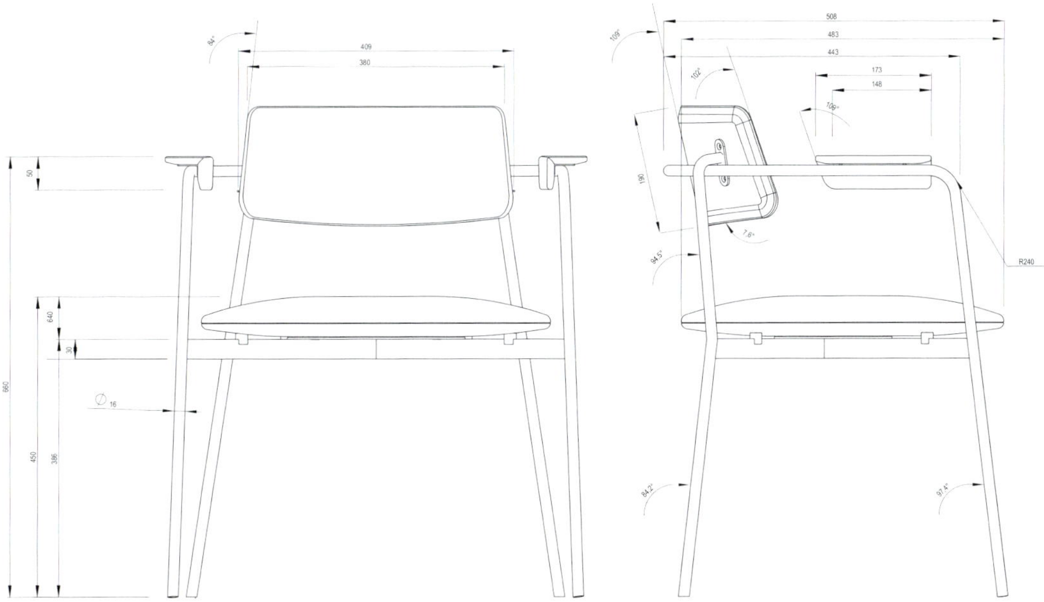

The furnishing of the children's department is important for creating an exciting and engaging place for the children.

A specially designed, modular media stand was developed by Scenario for increased flexibility for various exhibitions and collections. The basic modules in the media stand form the framework for all top shelves, inserts and additional components that can be assembled in different ways.

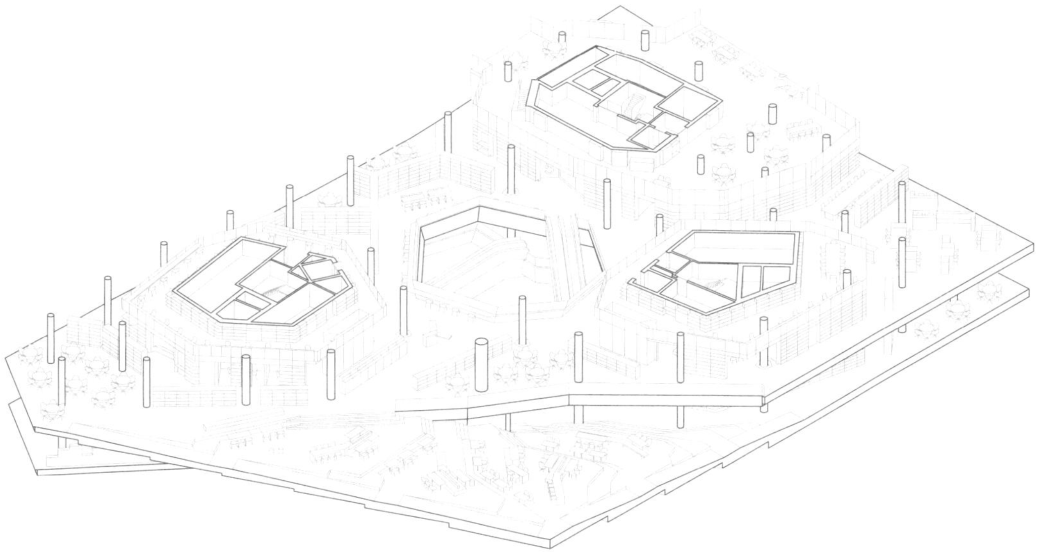

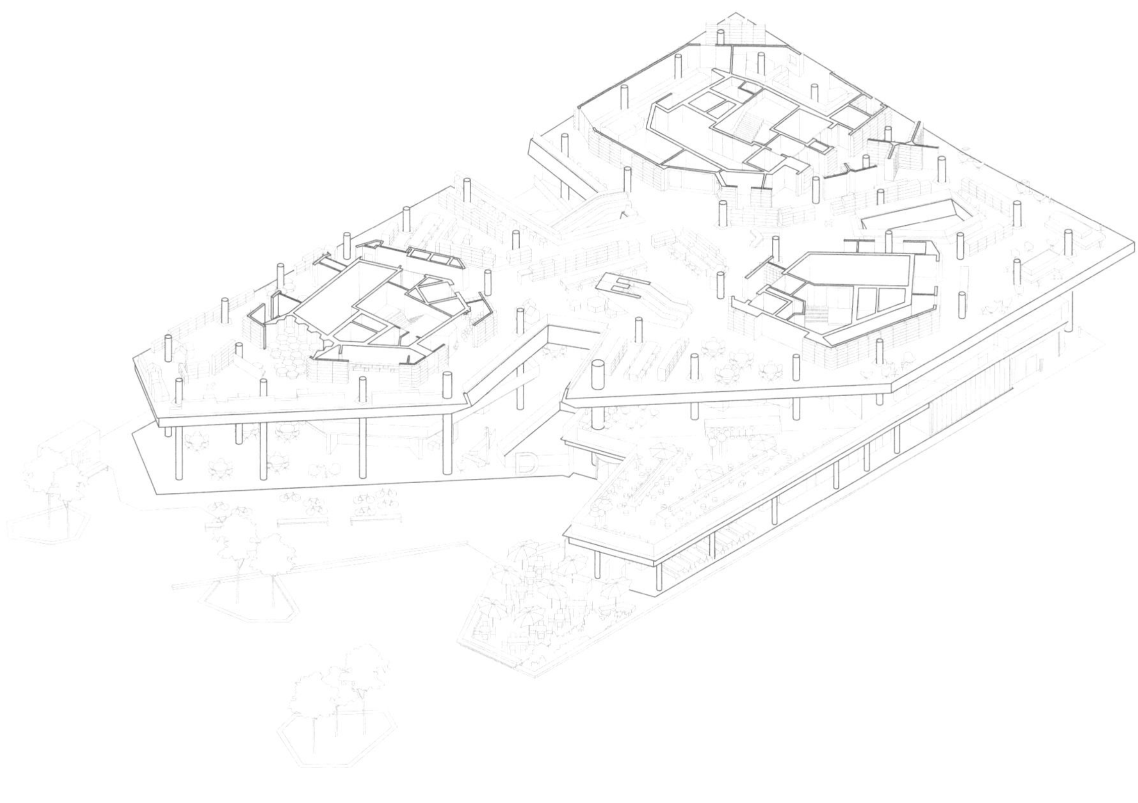

Axonometric views showing the building with furnishings.
Bottom section from the 1st floor, top from the 4th floor.

4 Epilogue – The People Move in

The new main library in Oslo's first year was a special one. The opening had to be postponed due to the Covid pandemic, but finally it opened in June 2020, more than eleven years after the competition had been won in 2009.

We wanted to design a library for people, a place where everyone could feel at home. The result was a large, continuous space containing a unique variety of places and qualities. It has become a building you discover as you walk around in it and where everyone can find their own place, exposed to the light shafts, tucked away on a mezzanine, or seated in a falling amphitheater with a view over the Oslo Fjord. It has become a library with a human scale within a larger dimension. A vibrant building that also offers areas for contemplation and tranquility.

Although the building is designed and planned around human activity, the three book towers or "shining cores" ensure that you still feel that you are in a library. The book is still present, and in many ways more than before. Now as much as 80 percent of the media collection is available to users of the library, in contrast to the abandoned library at Hammersborg, where only 20 percent was available, with the rest stacked away in inaccessible archives. Now the books are present in a way that supports human activity and helps to create a concentrated and contemplative atmosphere, which is still one of the qualities we seek in a library.

When the building opened, it was immediately put to use, and the people of Oslo quickly found themselves at ease in their new library. There is little doubt that the new main library is an institution that holds a particular place in the heart of this city. The offers Deichman Bjørvika has filled this building with are unique and have redefined what one previously thought of as a library. As the pandemic led to periods of closure, the municipality prioritized keeping the library open as the only one of the city's cultural institutions. That says something about how important the library is to the city.

> Schoolchildren symbolically moved the first books from the old library into the new.

DEICHMANSKE · BIBLIOTEK
DEICHMAN
DE

Deichman Bjørvika
Åpner i 2020
DE

5 Site-specific Artworks

There are several art projects connected to the new central library. The projects presented here are the three permanent, site-specific works: a sculpture on the plaza in front of the building, an installation above the entrance foyer, and a conceptual project with a designated room on the top floor. The art in the entrance area is the result of a competition arranged by the project's own art committee, which also initiated a temporary art program that is now in the hands of a specially employed curator. In addition, Deichman Bjørvika invites various artists to do projects of unequal duration. These exhibitions can be viewed throughout the whole building, allowing young and old alike to experience art and enjoy the works.

Creation from Iddefjord by Martin Puryear

On the plaza in front of the library, as part of the Opera common, Martin Puryear has created a beautiful 7-meter-tall sculpture he has called *Creation from Iddefjord.* It is a soft imaginary creature that stands in stark contrast to the crystalline library building. In the same way as the library it asks to be used by going through it, touching it, exploring and wondering. The sculpture is made of chiseled stone blocks in gray Iddefjord granite, the same stone Gustav Vigeland used for Vigelandsparken.

"It can be reminiscent of a kind of being, with an organic form and a certain attitude. I wanted to create a hybrid figure in stone that could be experienced both with the eyes and through direct physical contact."
Martin Puryear

The sculpture is a gift from The Savings Bank Foundation DNB and is part of the art project Skulpturstopp.

Wooden model of the sculpture.

Artist Martin Puryear in conversation with workers from Johansen Monumenthuggeri in Sarpsborg, who produced the sculpture of 40 separate granite blocks.

Brainstorm by Lars Ø. Ramberg

Brainstorm by Lars Ø. Ramberg hangs over the library square just inside the entrances. The artist won an invited competition announced by the art committee for the new Deichman main library in 2016. The art committee was led by Per Hess and consisted of representatives from Deichman, the architects, the project management and the Municipality of Oslo's cultural authority. The work is a huge sculpture of neon lights in 20 mm thin hand-blown glass tubes, with a total length of four hundred meters. The glass tubes form an energetic network of meandering lines in yellow and white that extend across the square. They give associations to the movement and speed of today's flow of information where people from all over the world now can be involved in an exchange of thoughts that has the potential, at best, to crush prejudice clear ground for new and unknown insights. It is a work that addresses the library's function and serve as an image for Oslo's new meeting place for knowledge and enlightenment.

Brainstorm is one of the largest productions in the Municipality of Oslo's art collection and has now become part of the city's public collection. The project was realized in collaboration with KORO (Norway's national body responsible for curating, producing and activating art in public space).

> The neon tubes form an energetic network of luminous lines across the library square.

Lars Ø. Ramberg while working on the sculpture at Nordiske Neon.

Future Library by Katie Paterson

Artist Katie Paterson in Nordmarka to plant one of the trees that in 100 years will be used for the paper on which the unpublished texts will be printed.

Future Library is a work of art that unfolds over a hundred years from 2014 to 2114. Each year, an author is invited to write a text that will not be read until an anthology of the 100 texts is published in 2114. The manuscripts are kept in a specially designated room on the top floor of Deichman Bjørvika.

An area of Nordmarka, the forest immediately north of Oslo, was put at the artist's disposal. First, the trees were cut down in accordance with the forest's natural regeneration process, to be used for the construction of the designated room for the manuscripts. Then, a thousand new trees were planted, to be cut down in a hundred years (2114) and used to make paper for the anthology. Every year an author is invited out to the forest to participate in an annual ceremony in which the title of the work is announced, and the text is handed over to the art project.

We were given the task of designing the room for the manuscripts in close collaboration with the artist.

The construction of the room consists of a hundred layers of carefully stacked wood pieces. A narrow passage creates a transition and distance to the rest of the library. This allows the visitor to adapt to the light and atmosphere of the small room. Inside, the walls become a bench, inviting you to rest and reflect. Each layer of wood contains a drawer that will eventually hold a manuscript. The fronts of the drawers are made of hand-cast glass that lets light from inside the drawer into the room, so that the lighting of the room comes from the manuscript drawers and emphasizes that the texts are the soul of the room.

The artwork was developed for Deichman by commission from Bjørvika Utvikling and is supported by the Municipality of Oslo. The *Future Library* Trust selects and invites the authors and sustains the artwork for its century-long duration.

Illustration of the room where the manuscripts are to be kept. The room is built of wood taken from the trees that were cut down in the forest.

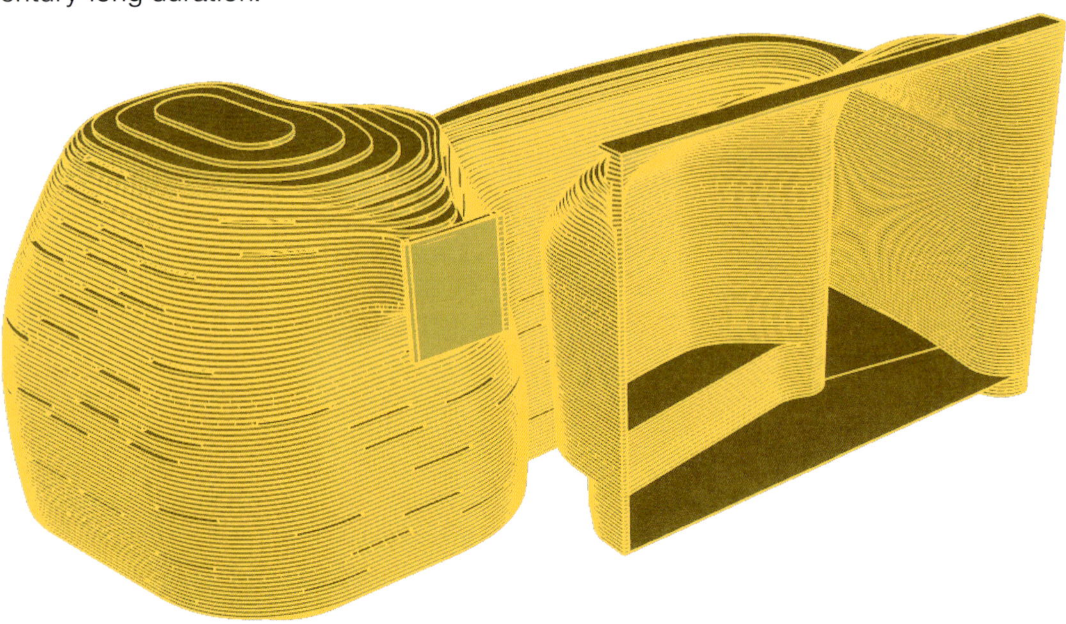

Plan and section of the room of the *Future Library*. The room is in the northwest corner of the 4th floor with the small window oriented toward the area in the forest where the wood used in the room came from.

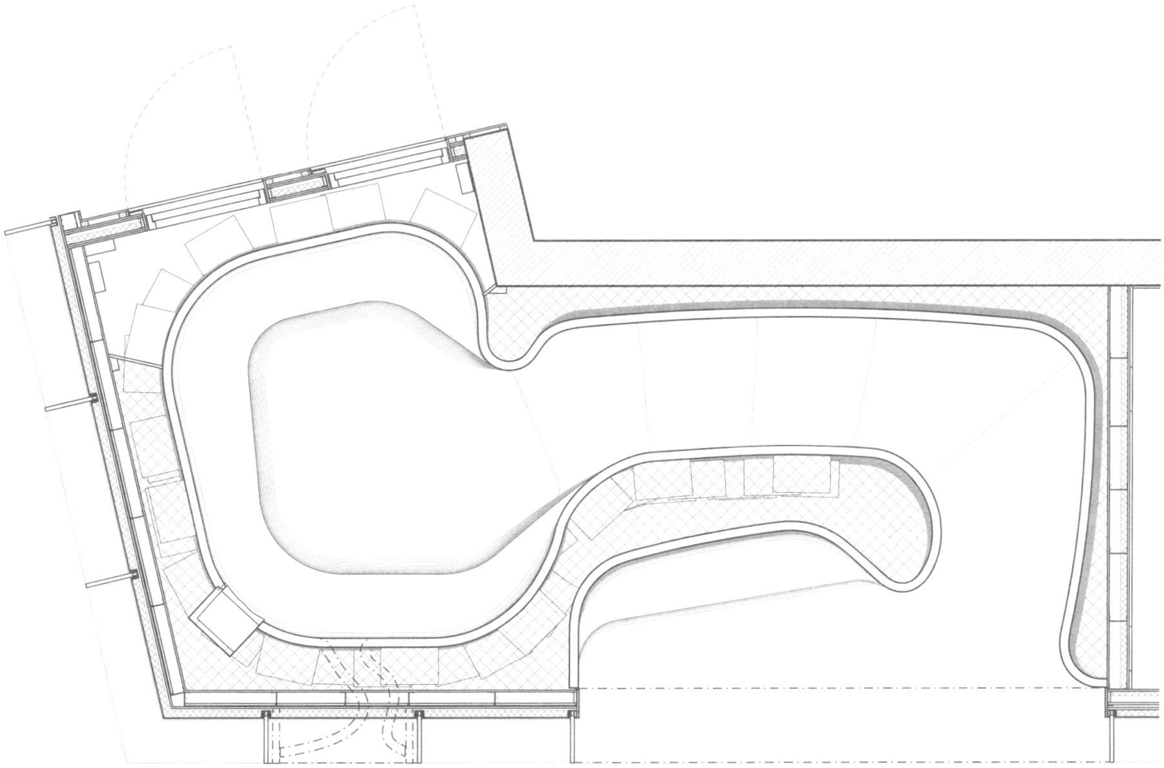

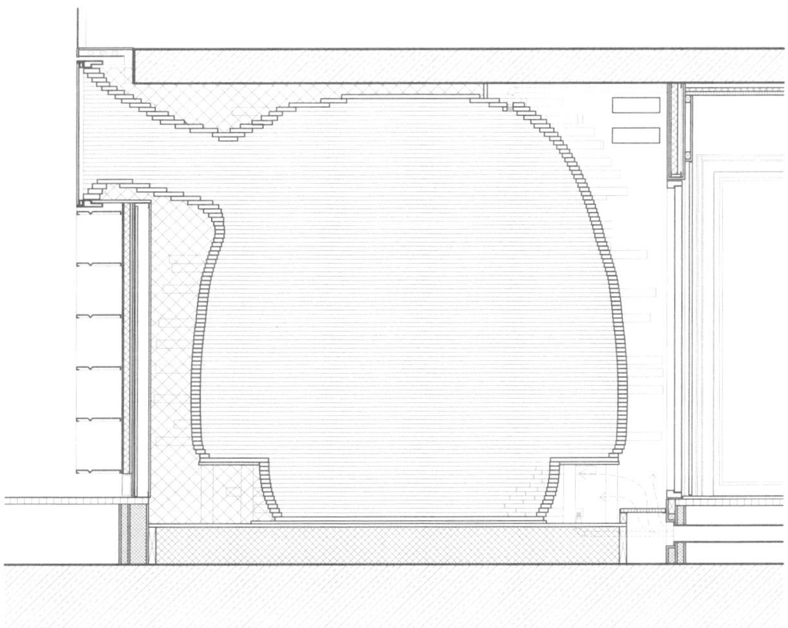

> From the narrow passageway where you get a glimpse of the room with the bench integrated in the wall.

Pictures from casting of the glass fronts at Magnor glassworks. The names of the various authors will be sandblasted into the glass as the drawers are filled.

Model of the room for the manuscripts; left looking down, right looking up.

6 Project Documentation

Deichman Bjørvika

Function: Central public library in Oslo

Client: Municipality of Oslo

Area: 19,600 sqm gross area

Budget: 2.47 billion Norwegian kroner

Content:
Six main floors containing open media collections, informal reading and working places, classrooms, meeting rooms, study cells, podcast studios, computer lab, maker space, instruments and movie screening stations, informal stages, exhibition spaces, multifunctional auditorium, cinema, conference facilities, restaurant and café.

Administration areas, including meeting rooms, staff canteen, closed book archives, maintenance workshop, storage, cleaning room, preparatory kitchen and cold storage. Underground logistics terminal for delivery of goods and books. Book sorting machine delivering media to all main floors.

Rental areas: shop and offices.

Opening hours: 08–22 / 10–18 HRS.

Media collection containing 450,000 units.

Total number of public seats: 1,200

Staff: 160, including restaurant and tenants.

Energy use: 75.6 kWh/sqm – passive house standard.

Material use: Core: Low carbon concrete with recycled steel. Shell: composite / glass facade.

Important dates: 2009: Architectural competition;
2014: Construction begins; 2020: Opening.

Siteplan

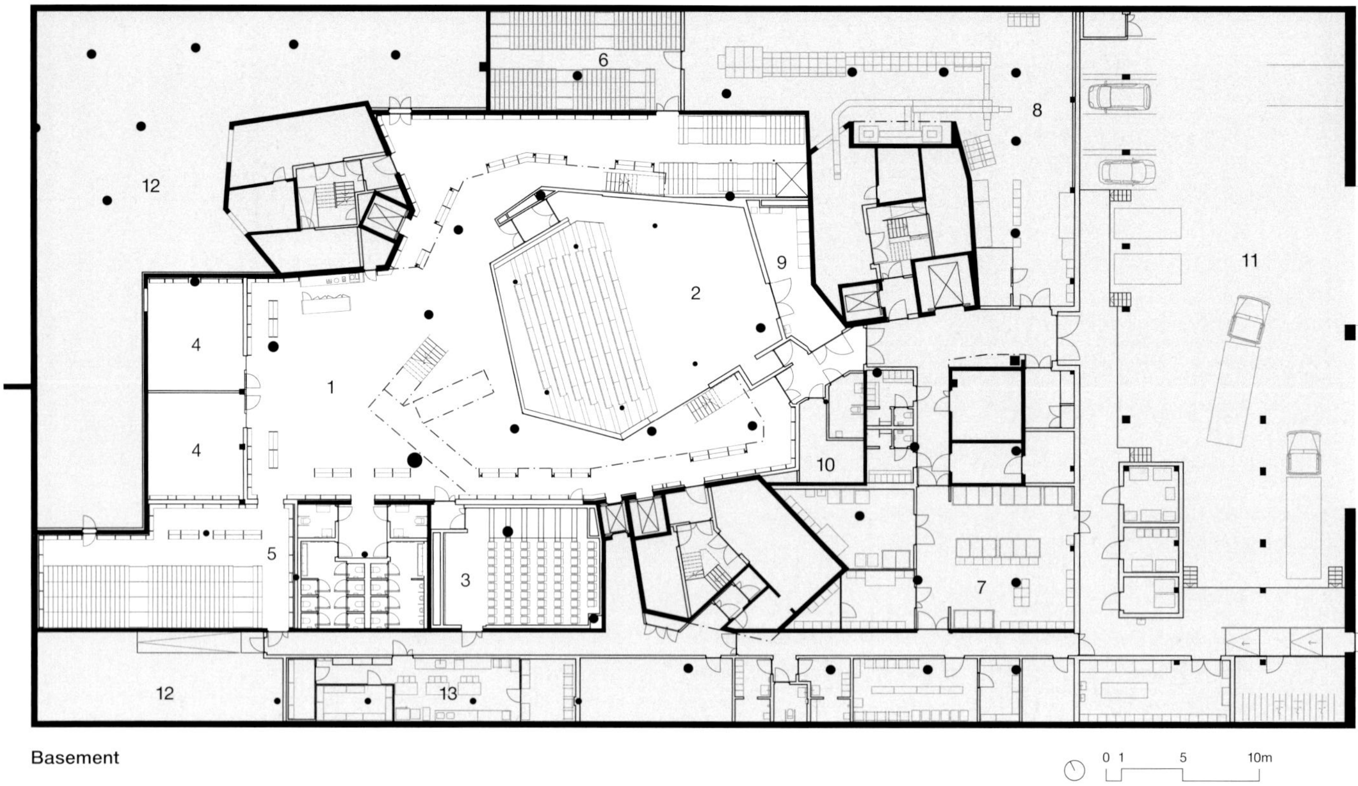

Basement

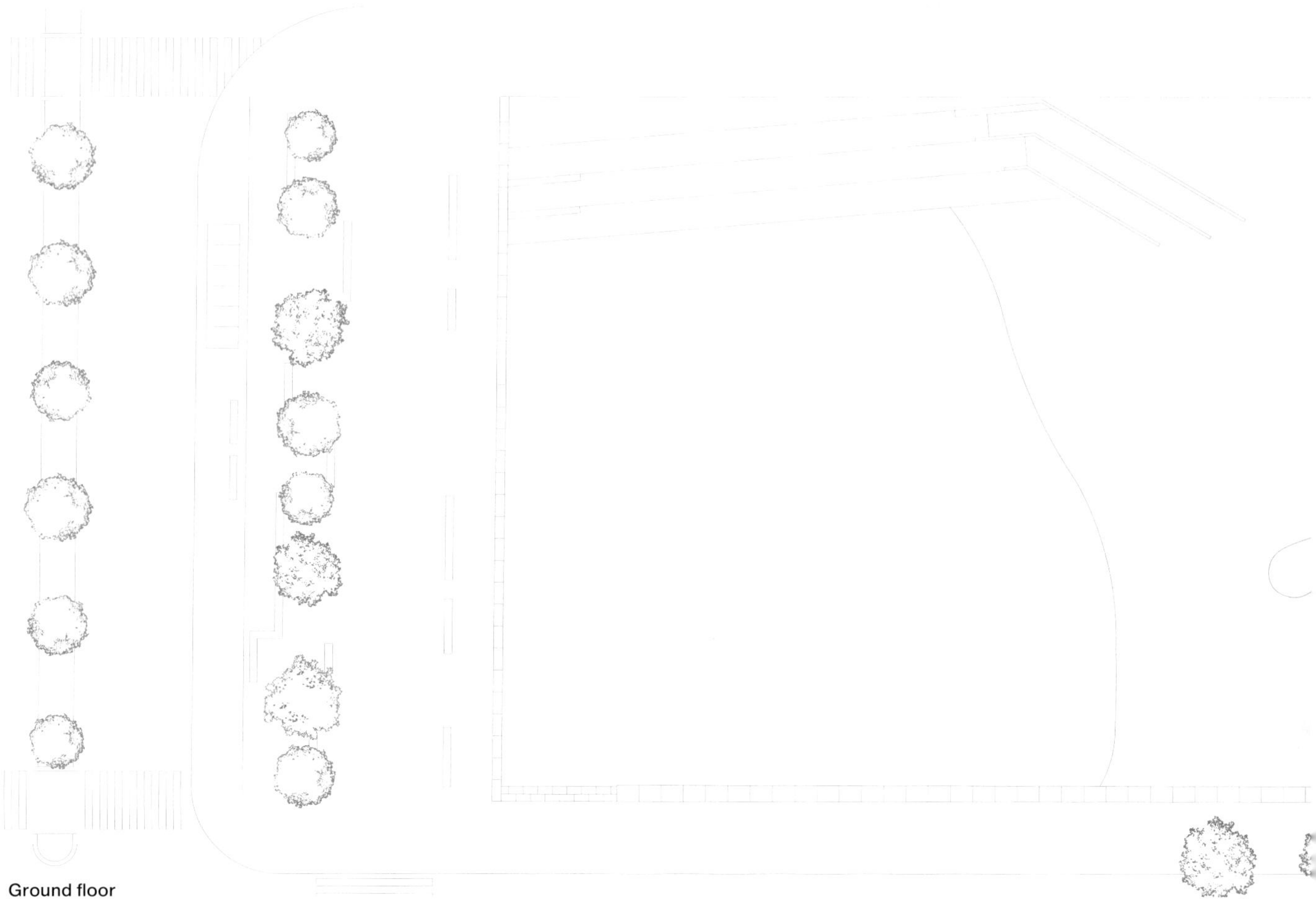

Ground floor

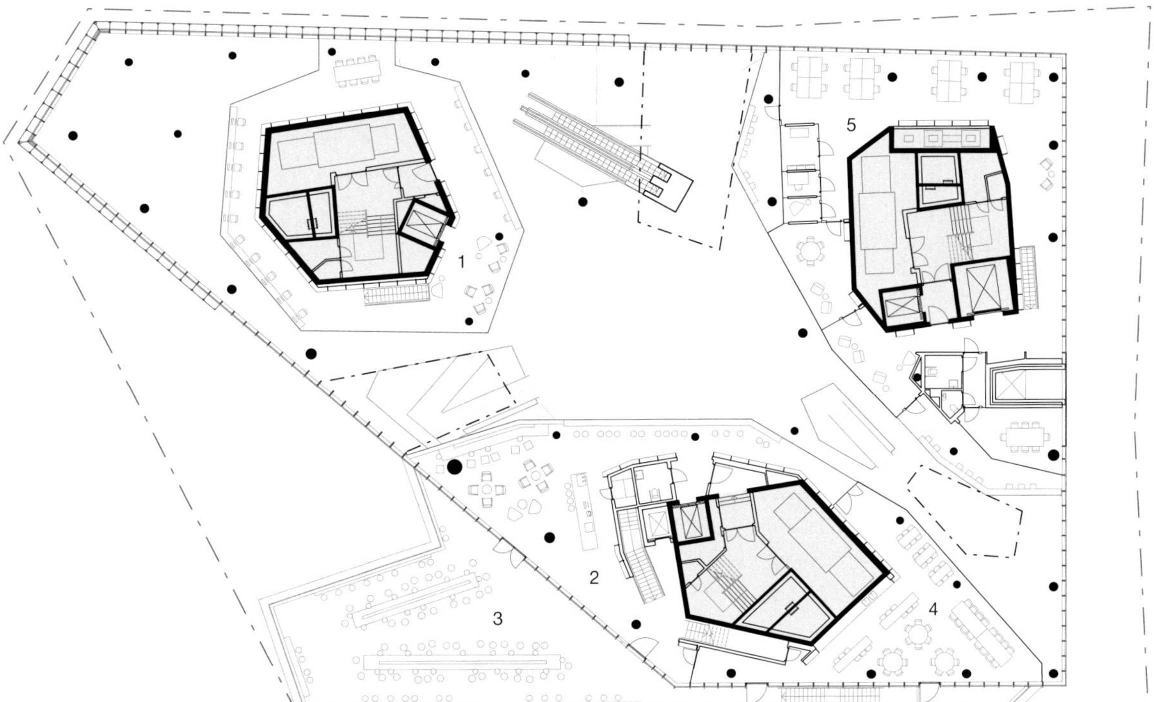

Ground-floor mezzanine

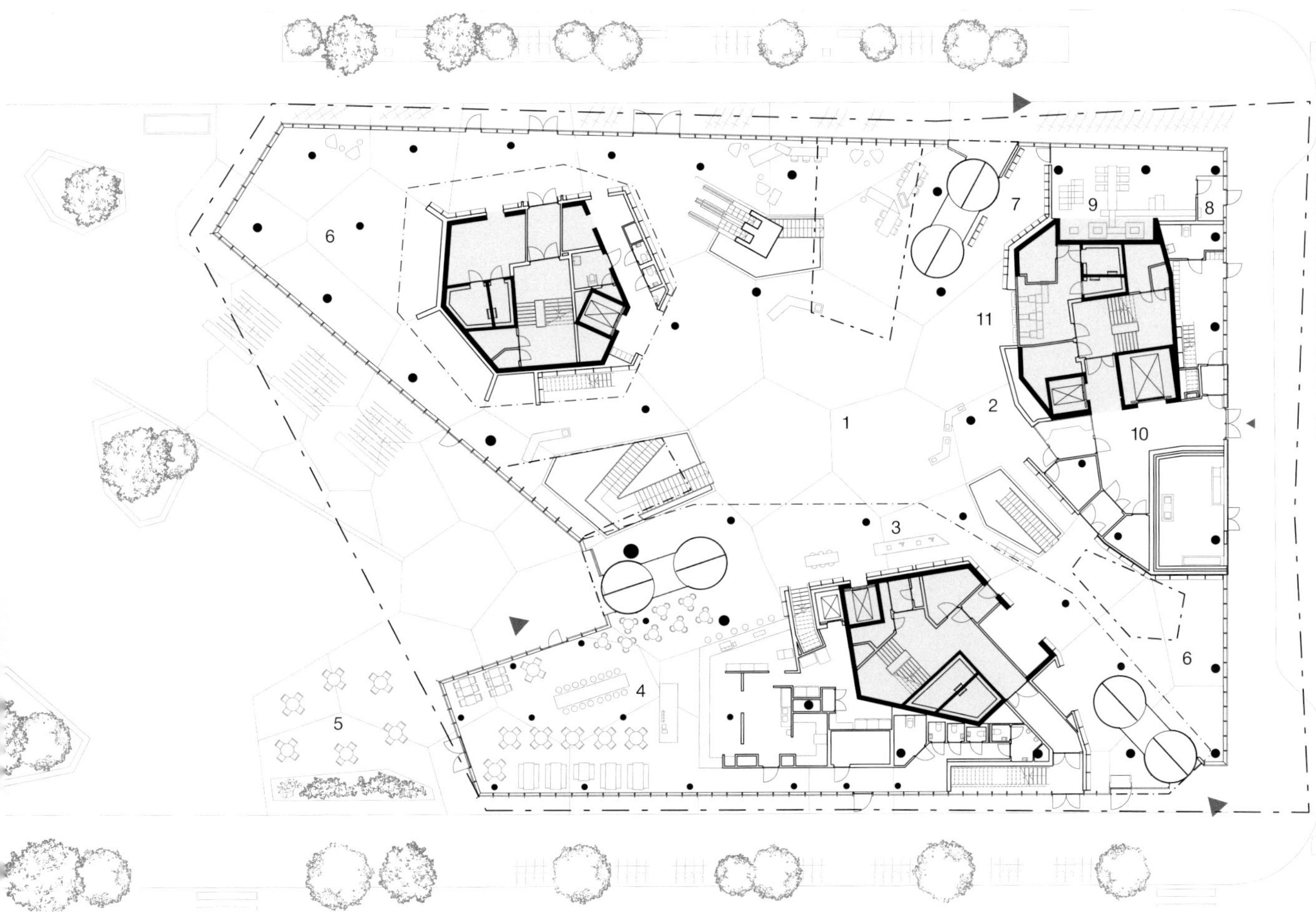

< Basement

1 Foyer
2 Auditorium
3 Cinema
4 Classrooms
5 Open archives
6 Closed archives
7 Workshop
8 Main book sorting and distribution
9 Backstage
10 Green room
11 Delivery area
12 Technical areas
13 Preparatory kitchen
14 Descent ramp

< Ground floor

1 Plaza
2 Info point
3 Help desk
4 Café / Restaurant
5 Outdoor café
6 Rent-out area
7 Pick-up shelf
8 24h library
9 Book sorting machine
10 Administration area
11 Hand-in machines

< Ground-floor mezzanine

1 Newspapers and magazines
2 Café / Bar
3 Terrace
4 Staff canteen
5 Administration

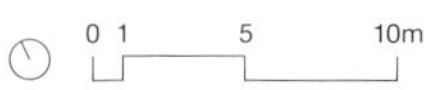

1st floor

1 Children's library
2 Play niches
3 Amphi / stage
4 Lounge area
5 Self-service café
6 Fiction
7 Book sorting machine
8 Exhibition niche
9 Info point
10 Micro library

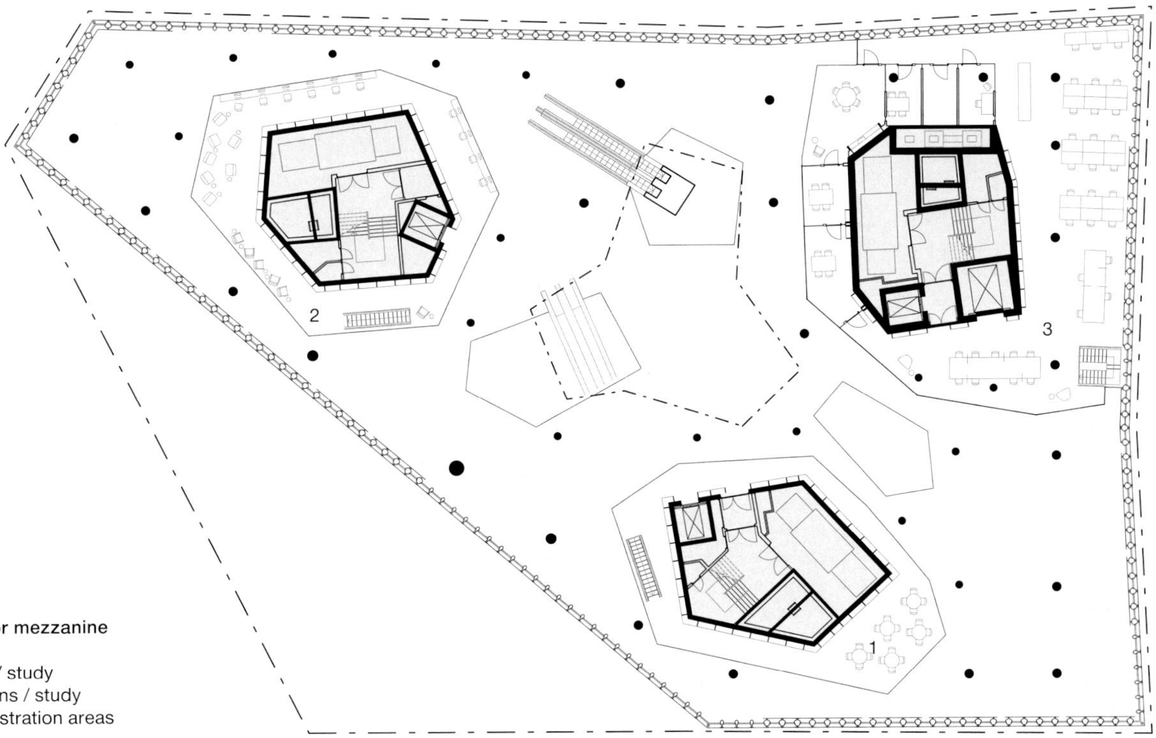

2nd floor mezzanine

1 Music / study
2 Cartoons / study
3 Administration areas

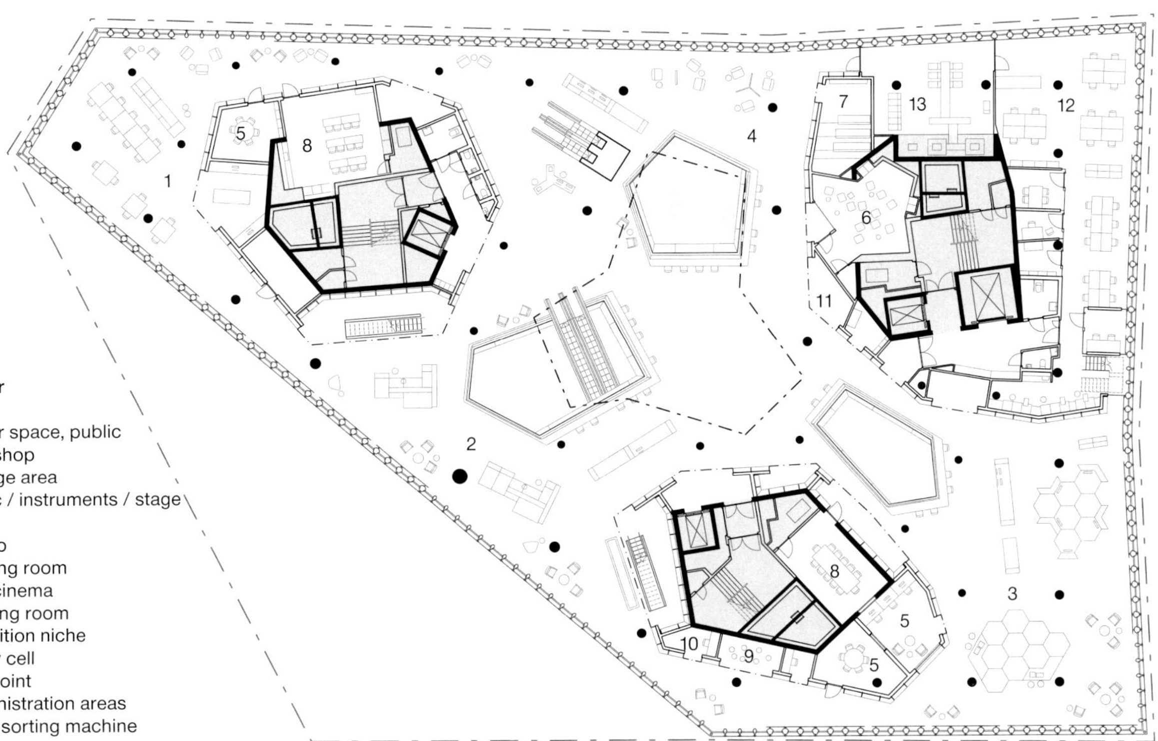

2nd floor

1 Maker space, public workshop
2 Lounge area
3 Music / instruments / stage
4 Film
5 Studio
6 Gaming room
7 Mini cinema
8 Meeting room
9 Exhibition niche
10 Study cell
11 Info point
12 Administration areas
13 Book sorting machine

3rd floor mezzanine

1 Study cells
2 Art and architecture
3 Social science
4 Science
5 Language lab
6 Study cell
7 Info point
8 Administration areas
9 Book sorting machine
10 Pop-up stage
11 Exhibition niche
12 Meeting rooms

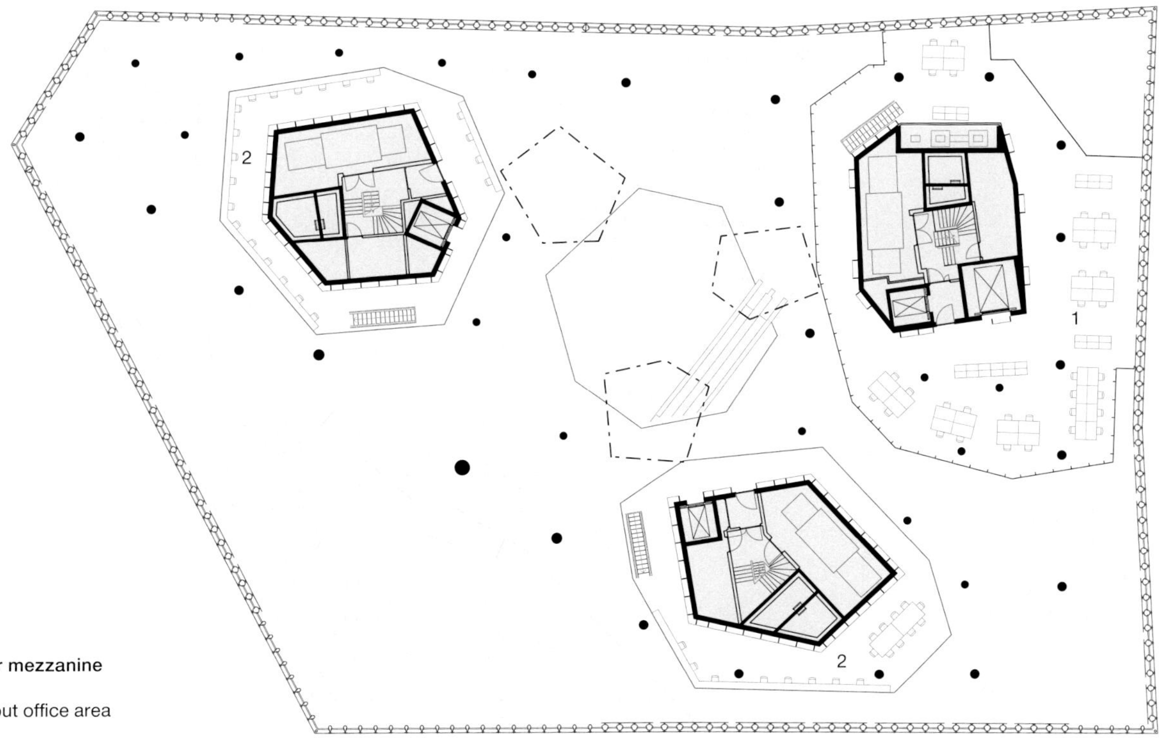

4th floor mezzanine

1 Rent-out office area
2 Study

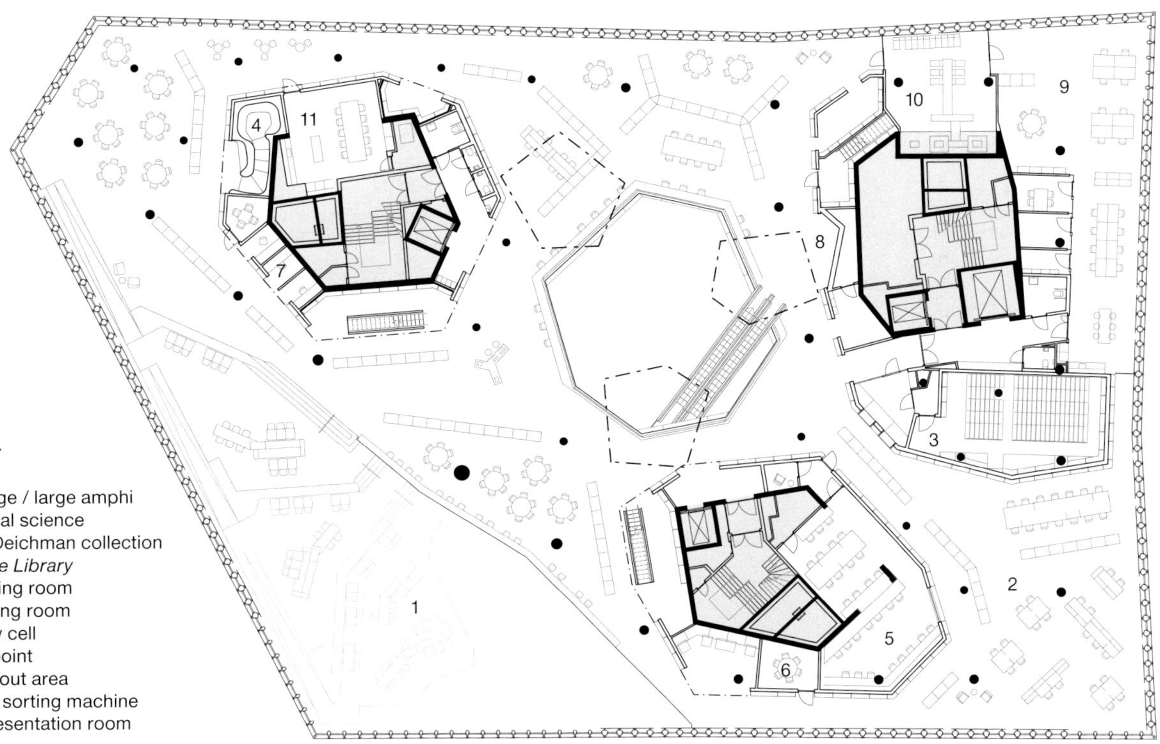

4th floor

1 Lounge / large amphi
2 Natural science
3 The Deichman collection
4 *Future Library*
5 Reading room
6 Meeting room
7 Study cell
8 Info point
9 Rent-out area
10 Book sorting machine
11 Representation room

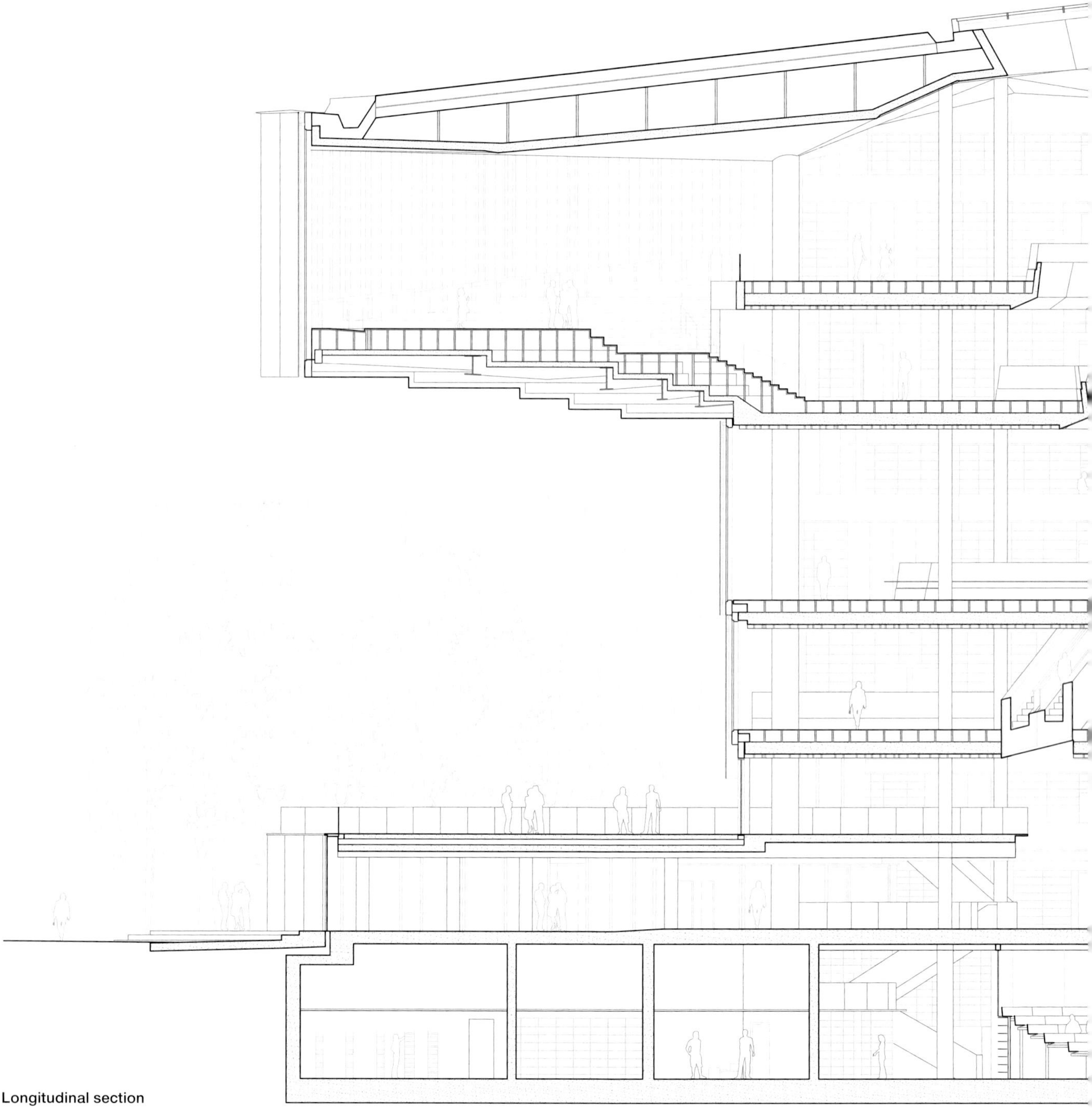

Longitudinal section

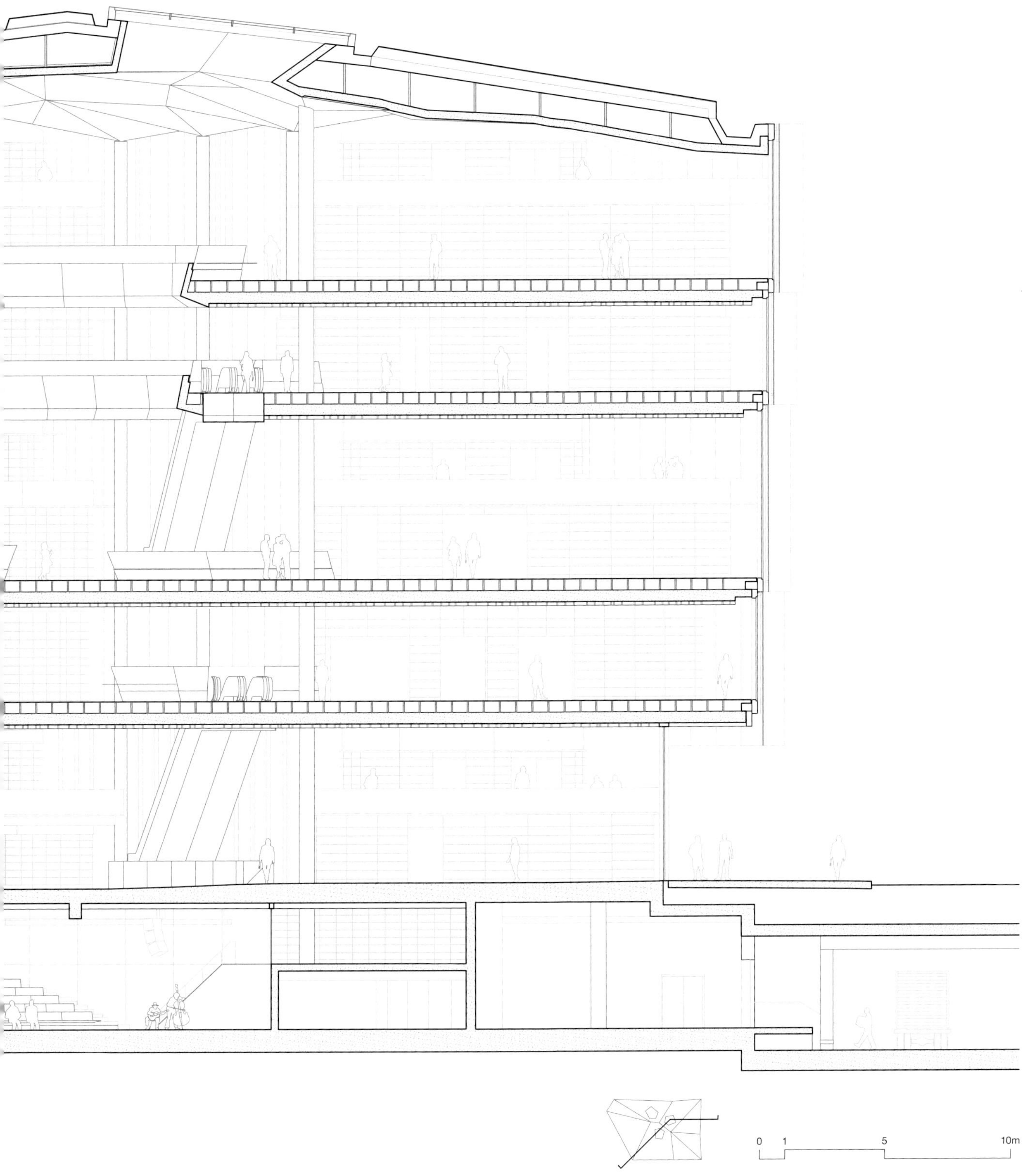
0
1
5
10m

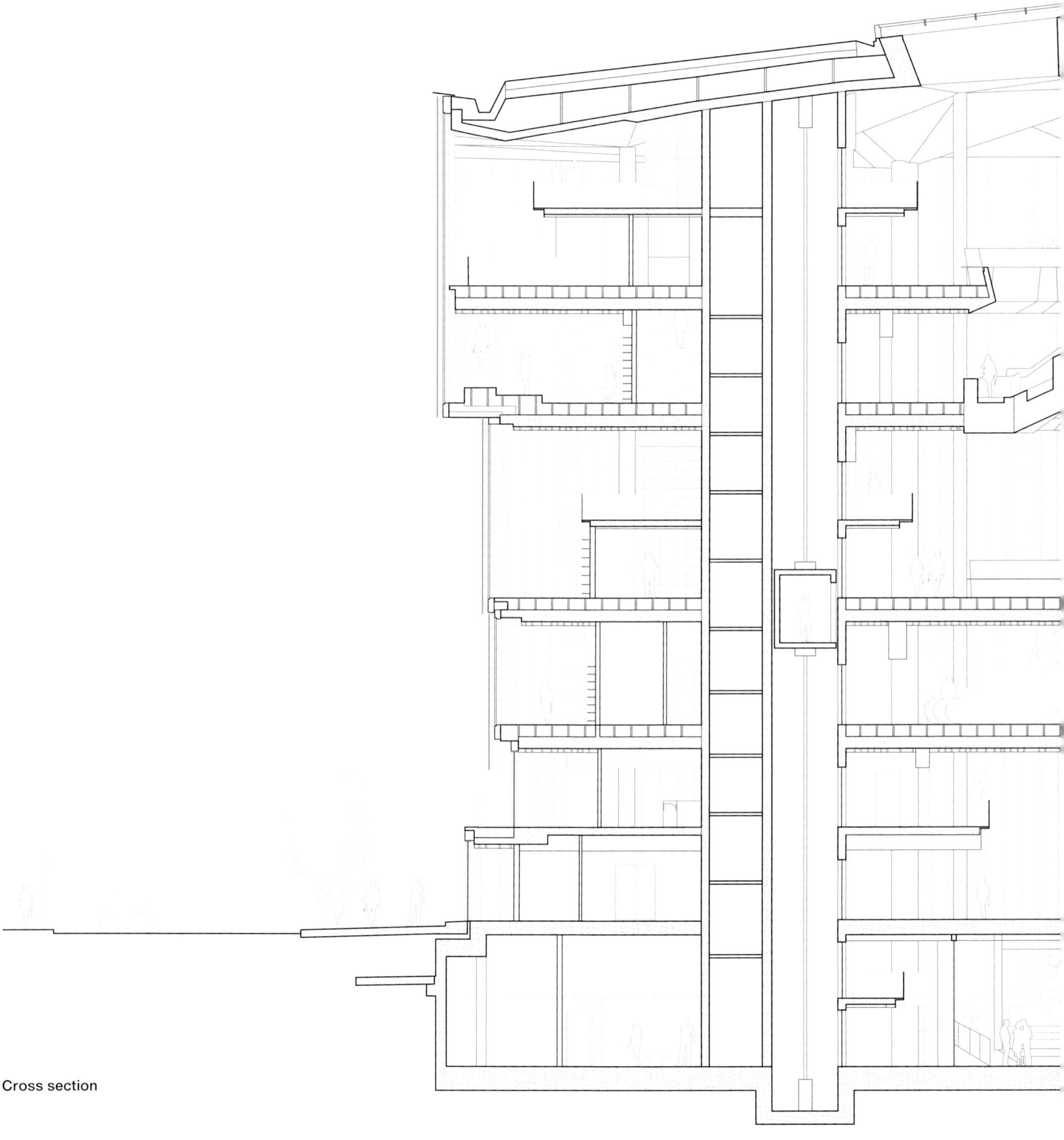

Cross section

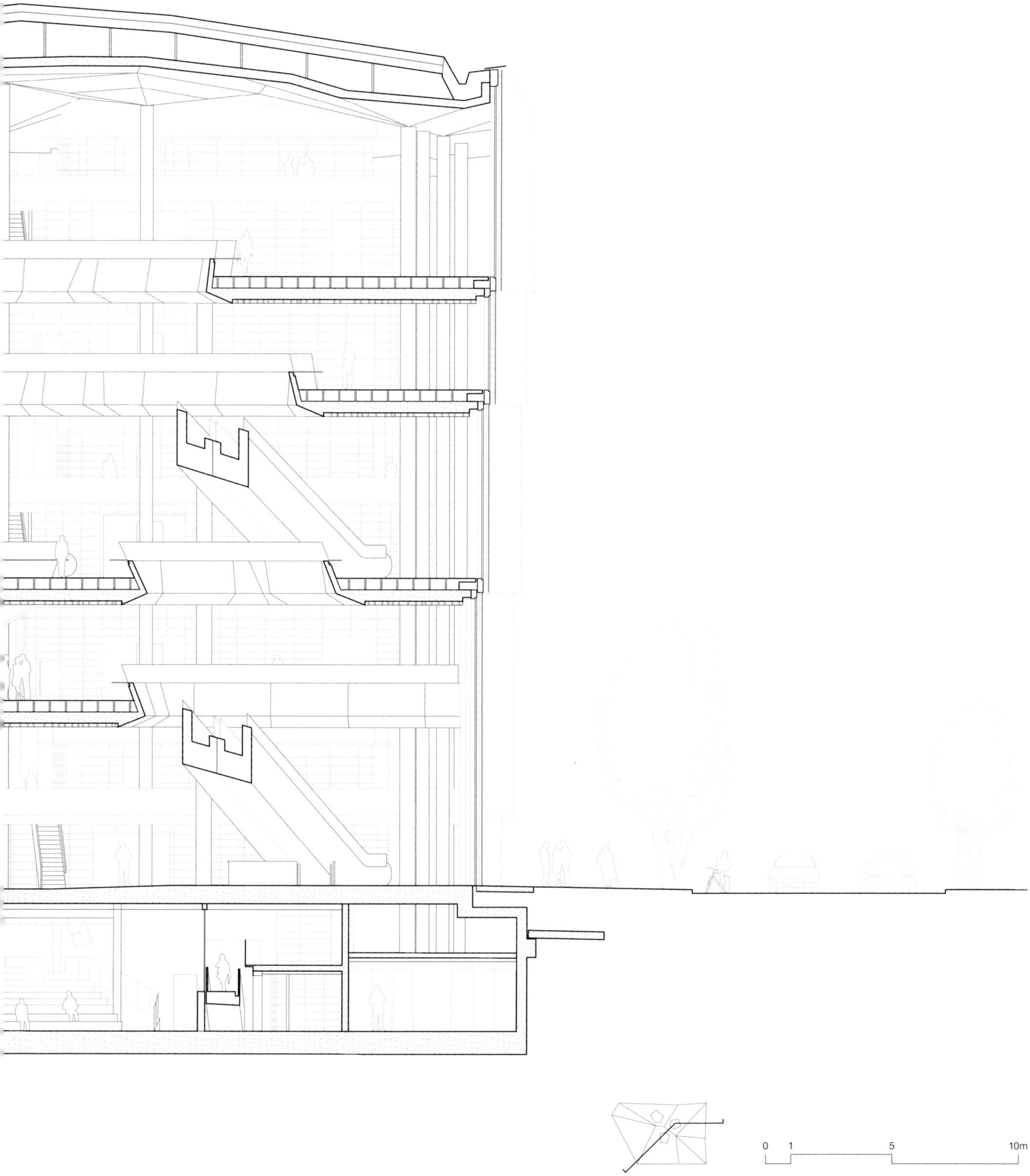
0 1 5 10m

HOTEL
Oslo Sentralstasjon

SpareBan

In a Novel Space

Niklas Maak

Look at them.

Two children, maybe five years old, with red cheeks and wild hair, run around, playing hide and seek. An old lady with steel-rimmed glasses and bluish hair sits in the corner of two bookshelves, talking on the mobile phone while flipping through the pages of Kjell Askildsen's novel Hverdag, *ordering somebody to buy "Tomater, eddik og brødsmuler" – maybe her husband. A young man, with big hands and an exuberant moustache, enters with a guitar on his back, apparently determined to start a career as a singer-songwriter. Another man shows up with a pair of torn trousers, asking for the room with the sewing machine. A young man drags his girlfriend over to a sofa. An old man sleeps on the couch next to it, a folded book on his belly, a confident, unconscious smile on his face. Two men are kissing in front of a window, admiring their reflections in the mirroring glass, looking at the fjord and the mountain silhouette that is about to fade into the darkness of the night. A group of ten teenagers stands in the middle of a 20-meter-tall space, staring with open mouths at the video playing on a mobile phone screen, while two women lay next to each other, chatting into their phones.*

It is rather rare to see all of this in a classic library. But this is not what you would call a classic library anyway.

I When I arrived at the library for the first time, the sun was just sinking. The building stood there like a monolith of milky glass, retracting its belly respectfully so the new opera house could be seen from the train station; it looked as if it could be folded up like a book. The upper part was dominated by a huge, adventurously cantilevering overhang that gave the library the look of something of a frozen rock, a pleasant cliff from which one must have a majestic view of Oslo's fjord.

At this time of day, many people gathered on the Opera House's sloping roof, contemplating the sunset, or trying to get as far up the slope with their bikes and E-scooters; a squad of electric vehicles buzzed by. The sun sank quickly, and when I turned around again, the library looked completely different: glowing from inside, that facade seemed to have dematerialized; it became transparent like a wet shirt, and behind the window, one could see hundreds of people reading books, or standing together, looking into the darkening night over the fjord, or lying down in the huge windows for a nap, with headphones on. Some children were pacing around.

II There is hardly a contemporary cultural building that offers such a massive surprise when entered, that is so unpredictable and different from the outside: While the proportions of the facade's glass panels indicate a regular interior with maybe four to six floors, the first astounding effect is the central core that reaches over the whole building height: Inside, the library looks much bigger, much more complex. From the outside, it resembles a building; from inside, a whole vertical city with narrow passages, big squares, panoramic terraces, playgrounds, and cozy houses formed by freestanding bookshelves of different heights.

Some of the library's most popular functions, such as the auditorium, the cinema, and an open-access library for children, are located in the basement; light from the auditorium's glass walls falls into the dark, narrow side alleys of this small town of books, drawing visitors' attention to the ongoing lectures.

Three structural cores bear the building, three light shafts run diagonally through it and form a monumentally large central hall at their intersection, a Piranesian swirl of smooth concrete which extends over all floors up to the origami of a folded concrete ceiling with, again, three skylights. Narrow escalators take visitors on a promenade architecturale from one floor to the other. The beautiful, pentagon-shaped foam elements, a necessary acoustic detail, give the building the appearance of something of a beehive with honeycomb patterns on the ceilings. Some of these floors have a mezzanine, forming cozy reading corners with very low ceiling height, like rock outcrops; then again, in the more open areas, you find working tables where students with laptops are writing e-mails or doing seminar work. On the first level, there is a vast reading corner for children that is used as a public playground. The next floor offers music, film, and comic sections, a mini-cinema and a stage, plus technologies such as recording studios and media workshops.

Further up, where the overhang protrudes, the house forms a huge flight of stairs. The cantilevered space overlooks the city, turning the library's upper floor into a viewpoint with panoramic vistas of the fjord and the green hills of Oslo. The building's spatial organization exudes formal and social permeability; from above, you can see all the different levels down to the ground floor, as if it was a mountain valley or a reef, with the most diverse creatures nestling in the numerous niches and corners.

III Some of the visitors were sitting on tables, looking down into the wide-open hall; others were lying on the ground, talking to friends, chatting over the phone, looking at films on their iPads, using the building like an extension of their bedrooms or living rooms into public space.

Claude Parent in his apartment, 1973, Neuilly-sur-Seine, France.

The famous French architect Claude Parent once wrote a pamphlet against the very idea of furniture; he installed slopes with soft carpets in his apartment instead, stating human interaction would gain in quality and affection when people were not forced to sit in a 90-degree angle on chairs, but could linger on the floor like gorillas in the rainforest, or recline like ancient Romans on a banquet couch.

When I walked though the building, hundreds of people were gathered there, some on huge sofas, immersed in their books, some engaged in a political discussion, sitting on a flight of stairs like in an amphitheater (they recalled the philosophers of the School of Athens in the eponymous painting by Raphael); just a meter away, a couple lie on the floor, legs intertwined, eyes closed, listening to music from earpods they shared, an unlikely display of a rather domestic form of intimacy; it was a Parentian dream come true. The outstanding acoustics of the library allow for people playing with their children and people reading or napping at the same time, simultaneously in a continuous space; a silent utopia. The library is capable of accommodating all of these diverse forms of being, of different emotional states from immersion and *solitudes à deux* to forms of collective experience rarely seen in a library building. Like in literature, small details change the atmosphere of this building almost imperceptibly; ceiling height diminishes, the floor changes from concrete to carpet, the dark shelves create an immersive mood of calm, while wide glass windows reconnect the visitor to the city and its epic surroundings.

With its thousand plateaus, reading corners, and vistas, it feels like a new form of a vertical city and a *Bildungslandschaft* (educational landscape) at the same time, enveloped with a composite and glass facade to protect it from the rain and Norway's harsh, long winters.

Just as literature captivates the reader with unexpected twists, the building amazes the visitor with magic tricks and an unconventional double use of tension beams: The engineers who were in charge of designing the structural support, suspended the cantilever with its glass facade from the roof. Its folded surface gives it more structural support, and, together with

Sala del Nuti, reading hall of the Malatestiana Library, built 1447–1452, Cesena, Italy.

Staatsbibliothek Potsdamer Strasse, Hans Scharoun, built 1967–1978, Berlin, Germany.

Salle Labrouste, Bibliothèque Nationale de France, Henry Labrouste, built 1854–1875, Paris, France.

the skylights, creates an appealing impression of lightness. In terms of sustainability, too, the library is a building for its time: it achieved a certification for passive house standards – a surprise given the amount of concrete used here; energy consumption is said to be as low as only 71 kilowatt hours per square meter per year. The ventilation, integrated in the floors, uses the thermal mass of the building, the concrete ceilings are cooled with built-in piping. External sun protection reduces the building's cooling requirement in summer.

IV The library is part of an astonishing urban recovery program: Until recently, roads and tracks blocked access to the waterfront, cutting the city off from its epic fjord. The construction of a car tunnel created space for new homes, offices, and cultural venues. The new opera house, with its giant sloping roof, has become Oslo's collective deck chair; with the new main library, Deichman Bjørvika, Lundhagem and Atelier Oslo have created a space that redefines a possible future city life even more radically: as a *Bildungslandschaft,* an educational landscape.

Except from some single early attempts to make knowledge available to a broader audience – among others in the 1447 Malatestians Library in Cesena, Italy – libraries have mostly been spaces of seclusion, accessible only to a privileged few. From the collection of manuscripts in Ancient Egypt and medieval France's monasteries to the great temples of knowledge production, like the Bibliothèque Nationale in Paris with its iconically modern Salle Labrouste, they were spaces of research, closed to the grand public.

Only in the eighteenth and even more throughout the nineteenth centuries, reformers like the archeologist Karl B. Preusker or Friedrich von Raumer imported the concept of the public library from America; Britain's Public Libraries Act made literature and education accessible to every citizen.

V Deichman, founded in 1785 by Carl Deichman, who had made his fortune in ironworks, was an early precursor to modern public libraries. The concept of the library as an educational space and form of countermodel

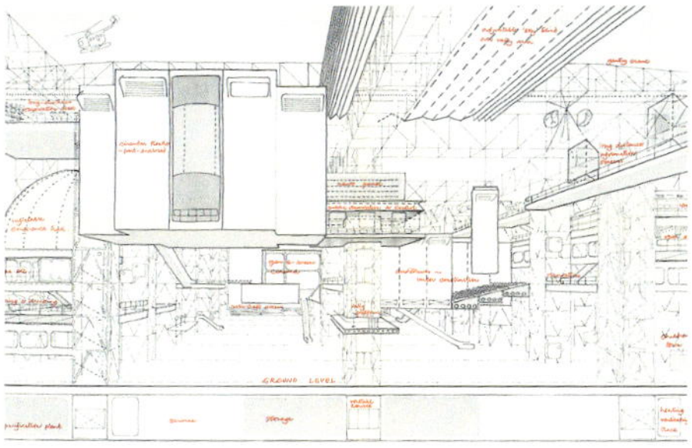

Hansabücherei, Werner Düttmann, built 1957, Berlin, Germany.

Bibliothèque Kandinsky, Centre Pompidou, Renzo Piano/Richard Rogers, built 1971–1977, Library opened 2002, Paris, France.

Fun Palace, Cedric Price and Joan Littlewood, 1964.

New Babylon, Constant Nieuwenhuys, 1959–1974.

to a public space shaped by commercial activities and interest became relevant in Europe only after the Second World War.

In Germany, the libraries designed by Werner Düttmann and Hans Scharoun were part of the democratic reeducation program after twelve years of National Socialist propaganda. Düttmann's library in the Hansa-Viertel of 1957 was a mat scheme pavilion with reading rooms and bookshelves oriented around an internal courtyard where people from the neighborhood could come together, grab a Hardoy Butterfly Chair and feel as if they were sitting in a luxurious, Palm Springs–style private bungalow. Düttmann's library was something unseen: a space that combined a domestic typology with public use. Traces of this play with paradoxical spatial atmospheres can be found also in Oslo's new library.

In France and other countries, the concept of these small town libraries was part of an effort to make education accessible to every citizen regardless of his or her socioeconomic status. The Centre Pompidou, a "culture machine" with museums, libraries, film studios, and workshops, was only the most spectacular iteration of these efforts. Its design owed much to the concept of Cedric Price's 1964 Fun Palace for Joan Littlewood, a never-built, yet highly influential proposal for an experimental stage; and Constant's New Babylon, a phantasmagory of what public space could look like at a moment when work would be increasingly robotized, and people would be able to spend their time wandering endlessly around on a labyrinthine structure, experiencing new things and exposing themselves to unknown sensations.

New Babylon referred also to the ancient concept of the Museion – which in ancient Greece designated not a single temple but a district of several buildings and gardens, a city of fictions and encounters with foreigners, where one could linger and meet storytellers and actors and other artists. Constant imagined a moment when, thanks to robotization, all forms of estranged labor would be abolished and people could dedicate themselves to what the Ancient Romans framed as *otium* – which only much later was slandered by Pietists as idleness.

Seattle Central Library, Rem Kohlhaas/OMA, built 2002–2004, Seattle, United States.

Otium did not only designate a temporary time of leisure and relaxation, but ways of dedicating one's time to meaningful things – eating with friends, reading, taking care of oneself, and also to the production of knowledge, insights, and even sustainable objects; producers of these objects were not driven by highest output and maximizing profit but by the quality and the joy in making and later using these objects. The counterconcept to *otium* was its literal negation, the *nec-otium,* which survives in today's word *negotiation,* the world of stressful and hectic public life, of unavoidable fights, the world of business and competition. Its detrimental effect to the bodies and minds is depicted in its being imagined as the negation of the good life: *nec-otium.*

VI In a way, otium and nec-otium mark a conceptual framework for societal priorities that are still, and maybe more than ever, of relevance today. After an efficiency-driven, exploitative late-twentieth-century capitalism with its well-known consequences for the environment and an aggravated split in the socioeconomic fabric of our societies, the demand for a recalibration of our priorities, from growth and expansion at any price, to a more solidary, sustainable form of living together and public well-being has become ever more urgent. In this moment, the library could become a training ground of a new form of public life. The early twenty-first century has – at the very moment when the book seemed outdated and under attack – seen a new culture of library building emerging.

Rem Koolhaas's 2004 Seattle Public Library marked the beginning of an effort to reenvision the library not only as a space of book storage and scholarly research but as a vertical city where people would spend whole days – a new Babylon with an umbrella of transparent glass folded over its spaces.

In the same spirit, Oslo's new library offers more than the 450,000 books it holds on its six floors: there is also a workshop with a 3-D printer, a 200-seat-theater, cafés, recording studios, and a room with sewing machines, much liked by young Oslo fashionistas, but also by people in need to mend their clothes. As a cultural hub, the library will also be a space of new forms of productivity after the end of shopping and work as we know it. Up to 3,000 visitors at a time can spend whole days here, meeting friends and strangers, reading or working, doing what formerly was done in a marketplace: exchanging information, producing goods, spending time in a space where, other than on most public squares, staying is only possible under the premise of buying something. It addresses young and elderly people and is accessible for everybody.

As with Koolhaas's library, the form does not want to convey an idea of regular beauty but of enormous energies; both buildings are energograms, situationist machines producing social energies. As in classic avant-garde paintings, the torsion of the three light shafts intensifies the perception of the building; the building's inner organs twist and turn and drag the visitor into ever new spaces and views.

The library becomes a new hybrid, a space of fictionalization, where experiencing other possible worlds in the act of reading and new forms of urban life blend into each other. The Oslo library, its giant hall with its velvety concrete that reminds one at some point of the brutalist churches of Gottfried Böhm, is a cathedral for the belief in a new form of spending time and living together, a structure responding to the ecological, but above all social and demographic challenges of our time.

VII Recent research proves that there is a growing demand for these counterspaces: In only four years, the old Deichman experienced an increase of 43 percent in visitor numbers; the new one is supposed to accommodate 2 million visitors per annum. According to an analysis of London's Tate Modern, more and more young people spend more than three hours in the museum – not necessarily to contemplate art but to meet friends, produce TikTok films, watch movies, play, and use the lobby as a collective living room.

In the summer, the building opens up and seems to push out something shaped like an ice floe under its cantilevered roof – a triangular restaurant with a roof terrace. In the winter, the building becomes a Noah's Ark that provides shelter to the life happening outside on a summer day; in the cantilevered sky lounge, people can enjoy the sun over the fjord even on a bitterly cold day.

In the coming years, we will witness an unprecedented production of modern ruins: post offices are closing – banks too – and especially after Covid, it is becoming apparent that more and more companies are enouraging their employees to work from home. At the same time, online shopping is on the rise; as a consequence, even the shopping mall, which was once accused of destroying the old city center and its commercial structures, is now becoming an endangered species itself. Work and consumption, the two factors that have shaped the cityscape and its social rituals for centuries, are disappearing from the urban realm as a consequence of digitalization.

But what will happen to the city and the way people use it, work in it, and live together in it, when the paradigmatic activities of work, consumption, and commerce shift to the Internet?

VIII Numerous designs for the smart cities of the future propose only gradual improvements and efficiency-enhanced variants of the existing city: using more wood than concrete, implementing smart things that will be connected, replacing cars with combustion engines by electric robo-cabs. But the axiomatic question is not raised: Where exactly will all these robo-cabs take us? What kind of "centers" will there be, and what exactly will we do there?

Oslo's new library gives a speculative answer – and is an example for intelligent axiomatic thinking. Axiomatic thinking means not only to improve the status quo gradually – by building office towers from wood instead of steel, by driving electric cars instead of combustion engines – but also to get you to fundamentally question the status quo.

What kinds of spaces would a society need if it shifted its main goals from full employment and accelerated economic growth to new forms of occupation, education, communication, and reproductive work? How would the city – its spaces, its rhythm, and its collective rituals – change if work as we know it vanished? And is the loss of estranged, low-wage labor, of shopping streets with mainly large retailers, really just a loss – or a chance to frame future urban life in a different way?

In the future, if digitalization gains are distributed equally and fairly and not privatized by a handful of tech giants, everything could change: how we organize our days, how we prioritize interhuman relationships, how we value reproductive work, how we dwell, how we create new forms of production beyond the parameters of maximized economic growth and expansion. This axiomatic shift would foster the invention of spaces that encourage different ways of spending time together, new forms of bringing up children, sleeping, caretaking, loving, and living with friends and neighbors.

IX But how to start a new architectural thinking? Architecture and language inevitably create a normative framework, and often it is difficult

Deichman Bjørvika, 2021, Oslo, Norway.

to escape. Sometimes we have to start with a critical look at the language we use. We all think we know what a "unit" is. We all think we know what it means to be private – we consider the bedroom a private space, the street a public one. But someone who sits on his bed with a laptop the whole day, Skyping, Zooming, trading, writing, sending e-mails, designing something, doing what traditionally was done in a marketplace, that is, exchanging information and goods: If he leaves his bedroom at night to get some fresh air, turns off the phone, and goes for a walk, is he really leaving a private room for the public space, or is it rather the other way around?

Maybe we need a new language. *Privacy,* for example, is not a nice word. It stems from the Latin *privare* – which means to steal something from somebody else. The act of becoming an individual is imagined as being born into a collective, and then stepping out and defending stolen territory, which is not a healthy concept. Maybe architects should not only worry about defending our privacy, but defend a temporary need for intimacy and protection, and also create an architectural framework for new forms of solidarity and togetherness.

The importance of Deichman Bjørvika for a future architectural history of our time may lie in the fact that it offers, as one of the few contemporary public buildings, compelling answers to what city life could be in the future and gives space to new forms of collectivity that could be tried out in these hallway's *magnificenca,* as Roland Barthes once called the liberating, emancipatory, anticlaustrophobic effect of a building's incommensurable size.

Oslo's new library is not only a library, but a workshop, a marketplace, and a drawing room. It creates spaces beyond categorical thinking and beyond the dichotomic terminology that we use to describe the city. Language can only approach it with the help of a paradox: It is a city made of books – and a giant public living room. It articulates, like the literature it houses, something new, the euphoria of a novel form, beyond words.

DEICHMAN
Hva kan vi hjelpe deg med?

Q
R

Barnelitteratur
Children's Literature
Skjønnlitteratur
Fiction
Skjønnlitteratur
Fiction

Teknikk
Engineering

Onsdag 24. juni
DEICHMAN
4. etasje
11:37
4
Del dine opplevelser!

KAOS

W

BERNINA
02

Studie 4.3
HROAR SCHEIBLER
TIDEMAND
ODDVAR TORSHEIM
Ulyzes

3M
MUSIKK - NOTER
Sheet Music
udie 3.1 - 3.2

Europas historie
History of Europe

Møterom TROSTERUD
Grupperom MADSERUD

CARL DEICHMAN-SAMLINGEN

Filosofi
5M

Tegneserier
Tegneserier

Arkitektur

Teknikk

CENTROPA

Robert Levins gate

HOTEL
OTEL OPERA

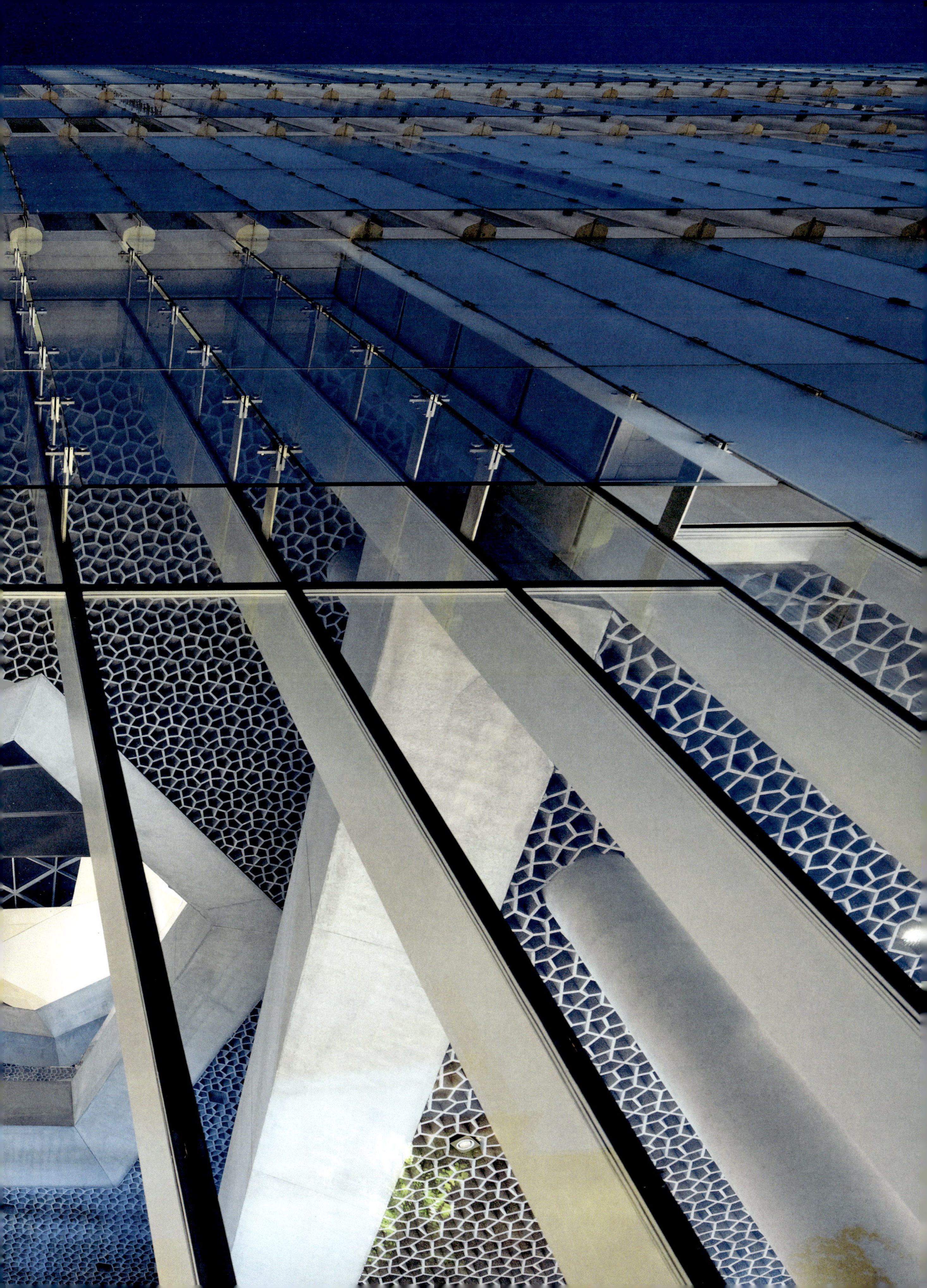

It takes a lot of people to realize a building like Deichman Bjørvika. We have received invaluable support from many enthusiastic individuals coming from political parties, agencies in the Municipality of Oslo, construction management, craftsmen, technical consultants and designers. And not least from the librarians!

At the risk of forgetting many, we still would like to single out some of those we have had the most contact with through the eleven-year process of designing and building the new main library. These are dedicated people from Kulturbyggene i Bjørvika, from the Planning and Building Agency, from Advansia project management, from OPAK construction management, from Bollinger + Grohmann engineers, from Multiconsult, from Scenario interior architects, from Asplan Viak and from the most important contractors represented by AF Gruppen, Lindner, Skanska and Roschmann – with subcontractors.

Special mention must be made of the employees at Deichman who have worked for the new main library and its conceptual basis for so long, and contributed with inspiring input and encouragement during the project development! A big thank-you to our employees in the two architectural firms who tirelessly and with great commitment have contributed more than one could dare to expect. And our families: wives, husbands, parents and children who have borne with us even through the most work-intensive periods.

Finally, we would like to thank Lars Müller and his colleagues for their great patience and commitment throughout the process of making this book. Without Lars Müller, this book would never have become a reality. We also want to thank Pax Forlag, who have helped us with the Norwegian edition.

Lundhagem and Atelier Oslo

Client: Oslo Municipality with Kulturbyggene i Bjørvika (now Oslobygg)
Client / user: Deichman
Project management: ÅF Advansia
Construction management: OPAK
Interior Architects: Scenario Interiørarkitekter
Landscape Architects: Agence Ter and SLA
Consulting engineers: Multiconsult
Structural engineers: Multiconsult and Bollinger + Grohmann
Acoustic engineers: Brekke og Strand and Multiconsult
Energy and environment: Asplan Viak
Security: Cowi
ICT: Rambøll
Adviser universal design: Universell Utforming
Technical description and cost estimates: Bygganalyse
Main contractors: AF Gruppen, Lindner, Skanska and Roschmann, with many skilled subcontractors

Architects Lundhagem:
Dennis Alekseev
Saulius Bulavas
Simen Storhaug Christiansen
Erlend Eidsaa
Nelson Ferreira
Quentin Le Guen-Geffroy
Einar Hagem
Svein Lund
Anders Melsom
Mariana Rapela
Mette Røsbekk
Graeme Sivell
Kristine Strøm-Gundersen
Per Suul
Vegar Voraa

Architects Atelier Oslo:
Nils Ole Bae Brandtzæg
Emmanuel Ferm
Heiki Fretheim
Bosheng Gan
Ola Wilthil Høgmoen
Ida Lenander
Thomas Liu
Marius Mowe
Jonas Norsted
Juan Ruiz
Adriana Sanz

Elif Shafak *1971, is an award-winning British-Turkish novelist who has published nineteen books, including her latest novel *The Island of Missing Trees.* She is a bestselling author in many countries and her work has been translated into 55 languages. *10 Minutes 38 Seconds in This Strange World* was shortlisted for the Booker Prize and RSL Ondaatje Prize, while *The Forty Rules of Love* was chosen by the BBC among 100 novels that shaped our world. Shafak holds a PhD in political science and is an honorary fellow at St Anne's College, Oxford University. She is also a Fellow and a Vice President of the Royal Society of Literature. An advocate for women's rights, LGBTQ+ rights, and freedom of expression, Shafak contributes to major publications around the world and was awarded the medal of Chevalier de l'Ordre des Arts et des Lettres.

Liv Sæteren *1944, was director of different libraries in smaller cities from 1968 to 1986, and she was library director at Oslo Public Library/Deichman from 1986 to 2013. Her main focus has been library development to meet changes in society, especially in information technology. This has included developing a new concept for library buildings and interiors. Her formal education is library school, political science, and public administration. She has presented numerous papers in international conferences and published several articles in periodicals. Sæteren was a member of various committees in the cultural field and has been honored with awards such as City of Oslo's Cultural Award, The King's Medal of Merit, the honorary award from the Norwegian library association and is a Paul Harris Fellow.

Niklas Maak *1972, is a writer and a professor in architecture at the Städel Fine Arts Institute in Frankfurt. Since 2001, he has been the editor for art and architecture at the *Frankfurter Allgemeine Zeitung.* He taught architecture at Harvard (2014–2020) and was a co-author and co-curator of Rem Koolhaas' research project "Countryside" and the eponymous exhibition at the Guggenheim Museum in New York. Among his latest publications are the novel *Technophoria* and the essay *Server Manifest: Architecture of the Data Center and the Future of Democracy.* He has been awarded the George F. Kennan Prize, the BDA Prize, and the Henri Nannen Prize, among others.

Einar Aslaksen *1982, was born and raised in Oslo, where he studied at the Oslo School of Photographic Arts in 2003–2004 before assisting many photographers in Oslo and New York. Since 2009 he has been working as a freelance photographer. After starting with artists documenting their work and collaborating with fashion magazines in his early career, he has been specializing in architectural photography in recent years. He worked with different clients in arts, design, and technology. Beside Deichman Bjørvika, he recently photographed the Kistefos Museum's new extension, named The Twist, designed by Bjarke Ingels Group (BIG Architects), and the Munch Museum, which opened in October 2021 and is located in Bjørvika, very close to the new main library.

Iwan Baan *1975, is an architecture and documentary photographer. His works are published regularly in architectural magazines and newspapers, among them are *Domus, a+u, New Yorker,* and the *New York Times.* He has worked with renowned architecture offices like SANAA, Rem Koolhaas/OMA, Herzog & de Meuron, Toyo Ito, and architects like Steven Holl and Zaha Hadid. In his photographs he focuses on the connection between architecture and the surrounding environment. Instead of isolating the built structure he embeds it in history and context.

Hélène Binet *1959, was born in Sorengo, Switzerland, and is of both Swiss and French descent. She grew up in Rome, where she studied photography at the Instituto Europeo di Design and soon developed an interest in architectural photography. Over a period of twenty-five years, Binet has photographed both contemporary and historical architecture, including the work of architects Caruso St John, Zaha Hadid, Libeskind, and Zumthor. More recently, she has directed her attention to landscape photography, wherein she transposes key concerns of her architectural photography. Binet's work has been published in a wide range of books and is shown in both national and international exhibitions. An advocate of analogue photography, Binet works exclusively with film.

Lundhagem
Lundhagem is an award-winning architecture and urbanism office based in Oslo. The office creates architecture, landscapes and interiors inspired by the Norwegian design tradition of simplicity, minimalism and functionality. The office's many projects are based on a sensitivity to landscape and dialogue between nature and the built environment. Lundhagem was founded in 1990 by Svein Lund and Einar Hagem. The office currently consists of more than 60 employees and is managed by five partners: Svein Lund, Einar Hagem, Mette Røsbekk, Per Suul and Kristine Strøm-Gundersen.

Svein Lund *1952, graduated from Oxford Polytechnic in 1980. Previously graduated as an engineer from Oslo University College of Engineering in 1974. Worked for F. S. Platou AS and Torp og Torp AS before he started his own office, Lund architects, in 1984. Founded Lundhagem in 1990 together with Einar Hagem.

Einar Hagem *1960, graduated from NTNU, Trondheim, in 1986. Also studied a year in Oslo with Sverre Fehn, and a year at the University of Georgia, US. Worked for Lund Architects from 1986 before he founded Lundhagem together with Svein Lund in 1990.

Mette Røsbekk *1969, graduated from NTNU, Trondheim, in 1994. Also studied at the Pratt Institute, School of Architecture, New York. Has worked at Lundhagem Architects since 1995. Became a partner in 2005.

Per Suul *1956, graduated from NTNU, Trondheim, in 1984. Worked at several recognized Norwegian offices before joining Lundhagem in 1996. Became a partner in 2005.

Kristine Strøm-Gundersen *1972, graduated from the University of North London in 1997. Studied architecture at the University of Glasgow, Glasgow School of Art from 1993 to 1996. Worked at several offices in London and Oslo before joining Lundhagem in 1999. Became a partner in 2013.

Atelier Oslo
Atelier Oslo is an award-winning architectural firm, which in recent years has realized several environment-friendly public buildings and transformation projects. The office's work ranges from major urban development projects to single-family houses and smaller installations. Atelier Oslo has a special interest in the relationship between architecture, man and nature. The working method is based on analyses, curiosity and interdisciplinary collaboration, which produces innovative and sustainable solutions. With inspiration from spatial typologies found in nature, and with a focus on structure and materials, they develop multifaceted and engaging projects. Atelier Oslo was founded in 2006 by Nils Ole Bae Brandtzæg, Thomas Liu, Marius Mowe and Jonas Norsted, and now consists of 15 architects with varied and international backgrounds.

Nils Ole Bae Brandtzæg *1975, graduated from the Oslo School of Architecture (AHO) in 2003. He also studied three years at the Academy of Fine Arts' School of Architecture in Copenhagen, and one year at the Cooper Union in New York. Worked at Lundhagem and architect Knut Hjeltnes, as well as the Norwegian Refugee Council in Sri Lanka before founding Atelier Oslo.

Marius Mowe *1973, graduated from the Oslo School of Architecture (AHO) in 2001. He also studied one year at the Technische Universität in Berlin. Worked for sculptor Bård Breivik and architect Sverre Fehn before founding Atelier Oslo.

Jonas Norsted *1973, graduated from the Oslo School of Architecture (AHO) in 2001. He also studied for a year at the University of Buenos Aires. Worked for Lundhagem and architect Eric Lapierre in Paris before founding Atelier Oslo.

Thomas Liu *1978, graduated from the Oslo School of Architecture (AHO) in 2003. Worked at sculptor Bård Breivik and at Jensen and Skodvin architect's office before founding Atelier Oslo.

Unless otherwise indicated, the copyright for the illustrations, plans and photographs is held by Lundhagem and Atelier Oslo.

t. = top
m. = middle
b. = bottom
l. = left
r. = right

© Einar Aslaksen: 111, 115 b.r., 153, 190, 191, 203, 206–207, 211, 229 t., 230–235, 243–245, 249–252, 262–267
© Iwan Baan: 113, 114 b.l., 155 b., 161, 180–189, 192–193, 204–205, 208–209, 212–225, 236–241,246–247, 253–261, 269
© Hélène Binet: 8–17, 29–35

50–51, 114 t. l. Candida Höfer, Deichmanske Bibliothek, Oslo II, 2000 © 2021, ProLitteris, Zurich
55–58 in chronological order: Karl Harstad, CC BY SA 3.0 NO, courtesy of Oslo Museum; Snøhetta; copyright unknown; Olav Olsen / Aftenposten; rights reserved; Lundhagem and Atelier Oslo; HAV Eiendom; Lundhagem and Atelier Oslo; Municipality of Oslo; Jiri Havran / Kultur- og idrettsbygg Oslo KF; Tore Kristiansen VG; Tore Meek / NTB; Jiri Havran / Kultur- og idrettsbygg Oslo KF; Copyright unknown; Jiri Havran / Kultur- og idrettsbygg Oslo KF; Jiri Havran / Kultur- og idrettsbygg Oslo KF; Terje Pedersen / NTB
60 Karl Harstad, CC BY SA 3.0 NO, courtesy of Oslo Museum
61 t. Copyright unknown
61 b. Candida Höfer, Deichmanske Bibliothek, Oslo III, 2000 © 2021, ProLitteris, Zurich
62 t. l. Map by Byens Opmaalingsvæsen
62 t. r. © 2021 Nyebilder
62 b., 65 Map data: Norkart
63 Bjørvika Infrastruktur
64 t. Einar Horsberg / Luma Foto / OSU
66 t. CC BY-NC 2.0, TwOsE / Flickr
66 b. l. © ulisses2 / 123RF.com
66 b. r. CC BY-NC-ND 2.0, Sun Brockie /Flickr
71 © 2021 Nyebilder
82–83 Tove Lauluten / Kultur- og idrettsbygg Oslo KF
85–89, 106, 144 Jiri Havran / Kultur- og idrettsbygg Oslo KF
93 Are Carlsen
97 b. CC BY-NC-SA 2.0, melina1965, Flickr
102 Bollinger+Grohmann
103 b. Doka Norge
104 m. l., 105 t., 107 RIB Multiconsult / Bollinger+Grohmann
104 b. Jørgen Rosendahl Halvorsen, Bubbledeck Norge
105 b. Rights reserved
109, 119, 121, 133, 135 Nils Vik
114 t. m. Daniele Ronca; courtesy of Baukunstarchiv, Akademie der Künste Berlin
114 t. r. Luis Orteo / Hemis / Alamy Stock Photo
114 b. m. a+t research group
114 b. r. Jean-Christophe Ballot / BnF
115 t. l. Rem Kohlhaas, Seattle Public Library, 2002–2004, © OMA AMO / 2021, ProLitteris, Zurich; Photo: Philippe Ruault,
115 t. m. CC BY-SA 4.0, Photo: meisho; courtesy of Toyo Ito Architects
115 t. r. Denis Esakov
115 b. l. CC BY-SA 4.0
115 b. m. Ulf Wallin
124 b. l. istockphoto / july7th
124 b. r. CC BY 2.0
129 t. m. b., 130 b., 131 t. Roschmann
144 Jiri Havran / Kultur- og idrettsbygg Oslo KF
154, 156 t. b. Scenario Interiørarkitekter / Gatis Rozenfelds
155 t. Scenario Interiørarkitekter
159 t. Tinna Ludviksdottir / Creative Commons
159 b. Stian Lysberg Solum / NTB Scanpix
160 b. l. © Martin Puryear/Courtesy the artist and Matthew Marks Gallery
160 b. r. © Skulpturstopp / André Løyning
162 Per Hess
163 Lars Ø. Ramberg
164 t. r. © MJC, 2014
167 © Vegard Kleven, 2020
197 © RMN – Gestion droit d'auteur Gilles Ehrmann; courtesy of Claude Parent Archive
198 t. l. hgm-press
198 b. l. Karl Johaentges; courtesy of Baukunstarchiv, Akademie der Künste Berlin
198 r. Jean-François Rollinger / Only France / Alamy Stock Photo
199 t. l. Landesdenkmalamt Berlin, Photo: Wolfgang Bittner; courtesy of Baukunstarchiv, Akademie der Künste Berlin
199 t. r. © Voyez-vous
199 b. l. Cedric Price fonds, Canadian Centre for Architecture
199 b. r. Constant Nieuwenhuys, © 2021, ProLitteris, Zurich
200 Rem Kohlhaas, Seattle Public Library, 2002–2004, © OMA AMO / 2021, ProLitteris, Zurich; Photo: CC BY-NC-SA 2.0, Flickr / Henry Figueroa
226–227, 229 b.r. Erik Thallaug
228 Gatis Rozenfelds

We have endeavored to identify all copyright holders and photographers. Should despite our intensive research any person entitled to rights have been overlooked, they are kindly requested to contact the publisher.

Deichman Bjørvika Oslo Public Library

Lundhagem and Atelier Oslo
Architects

Editors: Lars Müller and the architects
Authors: Niklas Maak, Elif Shafak, Liv Sæteren
Photographers: Einar Aslaksen, Iwan Baan, Hélène Binet
Translations: Jan Chr. Næss
Copyediting & proofreading: Keonaona Peterson
Design: Integral Lars Müller / Lars Müller and Ronja Burkard
Typesetting and production: Esther Butterworth
Editorial Coordination: Marius Wenger
Lithography: prints professional, Berlin, Germany
Printing: Narayana Press, Odder, Denmark
Binding: Buchbinderei S.R.Büge, Celle, Germany
Paper: 150 gsm Multiart Silk

Norwegian edition published by Pax Forlag
www.pax.no (ISBN 978-82-530-4320-3)

Lars Müller Publishers is supported by the Swiss Federal Office of Culture with a structural contribution for the years 2021–2024.

Lars Müller Publishers
Zurich, Switzerland
www.lars-mueller-publishers.com

ISBN 978-3-03778-650-5

Distributed in North America by ARTBOOK | D.A.P.
www.artbook.com

Printed in Denmark